The Pyramid of Trust

How to Go from Uncertainty to Certainty

Aimee Tariq
Lisa Fei
Imran Tariq
Tyler Wagner

Copyright © 2021 Aimee Tariq, Lisa Fei, Imran Tariq, Tyler Wagner

All Rights Reserved. This book contains material protected under International and Federal Copyright Laws and Treaties. Any unauthorized reprint or use of this material is prohibited. No part of this book may be reproduced or transmitted in any form or by any means, electronic or mechanical, including photocopying, recording, or by any information storage and retrieval system without express written permission from the author/publisher.

ISBN: 978-1-7351418-3-1
A Life With Health Publishing

Formatting by
AUTHORSUNITE
Authorsunite.com

PROLOGUE

The keys of trust are within your grasp—the ability to wield and fully tap into the power of this skill will enable you to reach the pinnacle of fulfillment and success in all facets of life. Every relationship, personally and professionally, including the one with yourself, requires the understanding of how to navigate the paths to establishing trust with the important people in your life journey. The following text gives you invaluable guidelines derived from the leading experts in every correlating field, from business leaders to life and relationship coaches, to psychologists and neuroscientists. Between this fount of indispensable information and guidance, and effort on your end to put it all into practice, there is no door to success or happiness that you cannot unlock.

* * *

Weaving the fabric of trust is a complex, intricate and worthwhile endeavor. To truly understand it, we must delicately unravel the layers and discover the significance behind the folds, while illuminating how trust has carefully webbed its way through every aspect of our lives.

"Trust" is a term that is used frequently, yet the concept itself is something that is scarcely appreciated for just how deeply interwoven it is with the human experience.

Most of us know what trusting someone feels like. Whether it's our parents, the government, or friends, it is an experience most of us have naturally come to give and receive throughout our lives, in different areas, and for different reasons. Many go through life without truly grasping the real meaning of trust, how to gain it, or how deeply it affects each segment of our lives.

Each time we take a breath, we trust there's air to fill our lungs. We trust our bodies know what to do with that air, and how to convert it to energy we need. We trust the sun will rise in the morning, and when the moon wanes, we trust it'll become full again in 28 days. But where does this sense of assurance come from? And what does it mean? Can we replicate it?

The Merriam-Webster Dictionary states that trust involves "assured reliance on the character, ability, strength, or truth of someone or something" and "dependence on something future or contingent," similar to hope. It can also mean "reliance on future payment for property delivered." So while the dictionary provides some answers, we know we're barely scratching the surface.

That said, there is so much more to the concept itself, and it is imperative that we understand it in its many complexities, how it affects our lives, and how to effectively navigate it, lest we risk the relationships that guide us and build us up both personally and professionally. We have to understand that the inability to build trust is of serious and perhaps even irreversible consequences. When combining these ideas about trust into a working definition, it needs to involve assurance, dependence, honesty, and loyalty, paired with the delicate balance of hope and faith.

Trust is heuristic, meaning that it is essentially a mental shortcut that allows people to make decisions quickly, rather than pausing to analyze every action, thought, and situation, referred to as "paralysis by analysis" (Lewicki, 2011). Trust prevents having to stop and analyze the possibilities of our decisions. If we were to be stopped in our tracks by every

THE PYRAMID OF TRUST

decision we were confronted with, we may never get anywhere in life, or perhaps those decisions would instead, be made for us. If everyone were to experience paralysis by analysis, nothing may ever get done. There may never be any trust in our convictions, and there would never be progress. Businesses would never grow, relationships would never thrive, there may not even be any society to speak of.

It has been long determined that human reason can only take decision-making so far due to the sheer array of possibilities and potential outcomes, which is why we need trust to expedite this process of thought, and why it is so vital to progress the expansion of interpersonal relationships.

In this sense, it is a bet, a suspension of disbelief that any contingent option would be better suited. Giving or accepting trust is a situation of interdependence, in which the trustor lends all action to the trustee, on the condition that the trustee adheres to expectations of the trustor.

Sociologically speaking, there are four types of trust:

Generalized: this can include trust in strangers and the unknown. This is the most important for society, as humans would hardly be capable of advancing if each person distrusted every person they met. This also applies to people you've never met, like national leaders for example. You've never met the president you voted for, but you may trust them nonetheless.

Out-group: trust in another group, ethnic, religious, national etc. For example, the confidence that two sister companies will act in each other's best interests.

In-group: trust in one's own group. Like trust that a co-owner of a company isn't going to take half of the company and employees and strike out to start their own independent business.

Neighbors: close-knit communities and interpersonal relationships.

The first stage of trust development is shaped by early years of childhood, according to German-American psychoanalyst and psychologist Erik Erikson. Success in the first years of development can lead to later years of trust and optimism, while failure can later forge mistrust and pessimism. "Success" and "failure" naturally translate to nurture or neglect - were the guardians compassionate and attentive, or unattentive or even abusive? In later years of adolescence when a child is more cognizant, upbringing also leaves a psychological impact on later propensity for building trust. This too, is based on the availability, attentiveness, responsiveness of the guardians. The end result of this is what is referred to as "attachment style", a psychological, ethological, and evolutionary theory on human relationships, which we will explore the breadths of in later chapters.

The key reason for trust is to provide the assurance that needs will be met, be they financial, emotional, sexual, or otherwise. Looking back at the prehistory of humankind, more simplistic versions of trust systems and relationships existed between people and groups. The men, who were trusted to hunt or defend the tribe, had to trust that their mates would protect their offspring, the next generation of warriors, hunters, and child-rearers. Even as hunter-gatherers, there was an understanding and trust that members of the tribe would protect one another against natural predators and neighboring enemies. Those outside of the warrior group would have roles of supporting the tribe, from childcare to gathering, from spiritual guidance to maintaining the health of the tribe. In exchange for the trust in full cooperation of the tribe, there was trust that bounties would be shared amongst all members of the tribe, rather than hoarded by those who attained it. This notion of trust would perpetuate itself ad infinitum, developing and evolving across the annals of history, in correlation with ever-shifting needs.

This state of trust which has been perpetuated since humans were little more than cooperative primates is widely reflected in our modern era in the form of relationships, professional or romantic. In more intimate relationships, a bond simply cannot exist without it. Trust and romantic relationships go hand-in hand, and the need thereof is hard-wired into our psychology. In this day and age, it is a bit more complex. Building feelings of assurance and intimacy, requires communication and consistency. This is not unlike building a strong professional relationship, in which communication and consistency are also essential ingredients.

Another factor to consider is independence. A term that is used often loosely by Americans, it is reminiscent of ideas about the revolution, the wild west, lone cowboys, and manifest destiny. However, the concept of independence as a whole in relation to trust-building has become more complicated as society has progressed. Independence is often a vague or lofty ideal, though it remains a significant issue in society. It is therefore the exact opposite of what individuals seek when establishing strong relationships.

In order for businesses to thrive, we need to be willing to establish community. Community implies a commitment to opening and fostering relationships. *Independence* is a word that is twisted to create a movement where being reliant upon others is not only a display of weakness, it's inefficient. Extreme forms of independence may convey nothing more than a lack of trust. This complete self-reliance might work for Clint Eastwood, but in our modern age, it's a hindrance to building the relationships necessary for thriving in life and can be psychologically unhealthy.

Imagine that you're trying to build a successful company from the ground up without help, guidance, or advice from people you trust. How are you going to build that company, provide a service for your many clients and consumers, or cultivate thriving business relationships, if you place too much importance on your individual independence? You may consider yourself to be a highly-advanced thinker or leader, but what is it really worth if you keep your skills to yourself? No man is an island, as humans are social animals with needs and desires.

We need others because our time is limited and precious, and how that time is used in tandem matters. Why divide both time and attention, which is perpetually in short supply, between the major functions needed to move a business forward, and the equally important supportive functions? Having to do both can be tedious and time-consuming, which is why hiring help, outsourcing mundane tasks, or even entering into a partnership is a necessity for expanding a business. By demonstrating dependence on others to fulfill certain needs, such as hiring someone to help with less vital tasks, we are freeing up our time to focus our mental and physical energies on things that will drive more growth in business.

The same concept of dependence can be applied to interpersonal relationships. We can't just always be working. There needs to be a dedication of time towards building our own relationships with friends, family, and our significant others. Then, if we place dependence on another person to share in the tasks and the time needed to complete them, we are able to fulfill a need of that person in turn, like giving them work and giving them the chance to feed their family.

A degree of dependence is essential to building trust, and so too is reciprocating acts of dependence. If you ask for a financial loan, or if you ask for your partner to take care of the dinner bill, that person's trust in you may falter if you don't reciprocate in some shape or form. They may be less inclined to extend a favor in the future. Likewise, if you return the favor, you have the opportunity to build that person's trust and confidence in you, therefore strengthening the relationship.

Trust is critical, for both building it up with those around us, as well as extending it to others. Trust is about more than the assurance that your romantic or business partner won't abandon you. It's about more than being confident that a figure of authority will behave as expected. Trust spans across all sectors of life, in all aspects and in every single decision. With this book, you will have more than just an understanding of how it affects your life so profoundly. You will have the key to unlocking trust in the hearts of those around you, enabling you to forge lasting, meaningful connections, flourishing intimacy, and professional relationships that will propel you towards profit and prosperity.

1

THE PYRAMID OF TRUST

UNDERSTANDING ITS STRUCTURE AND THE ELEMENTS OF ITS FOUNDATION

The Great Pyramid at Giza is a monumental structure that was built around 2560 BC. Since then, there were no man made structures that could even begin to rival its size and enginuity until the modern age. The pyramid has loomed over the desiccated sands of the Al Giza Desert for millenia, and has served as a proud and imperishable testament to the legacy of Egypt and it's pharaohs of old. There are few structures that possess such structural integrity, let alone among those so ancient. The Giza pyramid has stood the test of time, and may very well continue to do so for thousands of years more. This can be attributed to many factors, namely a strong foundation built to last.

This is not unlike the levels of trust, which build upwards in terms of personal importance, with a sturdy foundation holding everything together. From that which drives each of us individually to what moves society forward, trust compels us to build bonds with those around us and improve the quality of our lives. Without a strong foundation to hold this trust together, the structure itself, no matter how impregnable, will inevitably collapse into the abyss of uncertainty and distrust.

What does a solid foundation represent in relation to trust? At any level, it is like any other structure: without a solid foundation, it will inevitably crumble. But what is the so-called foundation of trust? What's more, what do these pyramidic levels of trust represent? Using the pyramid example, there are five levels of trust:

Blind trust: complete or near-complete suspension of reason in their respective public, with no guarantee of return for the trustees. The action of lending trust is practically impulsive and in the moment, as trustees become part of a greater mechanism led by the trusted. Examples of this include those who hold titles of seniority over a group, like an orchestral conductor, and also cult leaders, who use manipulation to come into a position "deserving" of trust.

Authoritative trust: celebrity, public figures of authority, experts, and influencers. With this, there is some use of logic, as reflected by public trust, along with a need for correlating values. Celebrities will continue their career, politicians will follow through with their promises, etc., in exchange for the public lending it's trust. What's more, they promise that they will not give further reason to distrust if trust is broken, and if they do otherwise, or if their act of betrayal was overwhelmingly heinous to begin with, their credibility will shatter and their career will fail. As such, building and maintaining credibility at this level of the pyramid is a must.

Professional or public trust: lending trust in the professional sphere calls for high use of logic. In regards to the investee, are they worthy of trust, investment, or partnership? What is the return? What is their track record with utilization and return of such trust? Likewise, when building public trust for yourself as an investor or your company, how do you do so? How do you choose to present yourself and your company to the public, with contributing factors such as your values, competency, credibility?

Interpersonal trust: referring to friendships, family relationships, and most importantly, romantic relationships. Sure, trust is important in relationships, but how important, and in what aspects? How does one build trust in a relationship? Again, we return to the previous level, the importance of solid consistency and a good track record. What's more, how does one rebuild trust that was lost in an interpersonal relationship?

It is also important to note that there are five conditions essential for building trust for any of these levels:

Competency
Credibility
Compassion
Communication
Consistency

These conditions refer to an exertion of effort towards building a relationship and bond of trust.

Competency

There are a number of layers to consider when ascertaining one's competency in regards to building trust. The dictionary attributes the term to ability, capacity, and proficiency, so we will start with explaining competency in trust by these terms.

First there's ability, or perhaps aptitude would be another term to use - someone's value based on how well they can build trust. There's a certain level of skill that goes into methods for building trust, such as being a good listener, attentive, open-minded, fulfilling needs and so on. In a professional setting, this also means being prepared and knowledgeable about your speciality. This implies being honest with yourself and others about what you know and don't know. If you aren't, real experts in the field will be able to sniff out a lack of understanding fairly quickly, thereby undermining your credibility (Harvard Business Review 2014).

This brings us to the next layer: capacity. In other words, there has to be a level of willingness to be considerate of the person you're trying to build trust with. This might take the form of exerting effort for them, being empathetic to their feelings and wants, or being open to making changes and improving yourself as is necessary to accommodate them. It's about a willingness to understand the other person and make the effort to show them that they matter. Professionally speaking, this translates to being adaptable. You may not know everything about your chosen field, and you should be honest about what you know and don't know. That said, you should also be willing to learn new aspects and be open to productive criticism. And of course, capacity also means exerting a level of empathy and understanding for others and their circumstances in a professional setting, such as giving ample pregnancy leave for example.

Next we come to proficiency. This is about more than just aptitude, but consistency and dependability as well. If you're an employee, you can be the hardest worker that a company has ever had, but if you only show up to work on time every other day, your work ethic will inevitably be called into question. The same can be applied to building trust in relationships. If you have a friend or a partner who can't be bothered to show up at your agreed upon time or when you're going through a crisis and you need their support, why would you bother giving that person your time when it is convenient for them? Why would you do the same for them?

We now have a working conceptualization for competency. It is a matter of aptitude, willingness, openness, and dependability.

Credibility

The next component of our foundation for trust is credibility. It may not be as important as self-trust on a personal level, though it is far from a trifling matter. Unlike self-trust, credibility is how the people around us gauge our value. It is the quality of being believed and trusted in which is why it is equally imperative for building relationships.

When navigating the world outside of one's personal bubble, credibility is everything. It is how we are perceived by the people around us. Our value correlates with the amount of trust that people are willing to lend us. How people you engage with throughout your life look at you can determine the course of your future and fortune in navigating and building personal or professional relationships.

Credibility is in your resume, your tendencies, your habits. Credibility is rarely developed overnight, and can be a rather arduous journey. It's something that requires time to cultivate, from building financial credit over the course of one's life to increasing credentials through years of experience or education, but the results can be rewarding.

Simply put, who would you rather perform heart-surgery on you, a qualified doctor with an eight-year degree and twenty years of experience, or someone fresh out of residency? Needless to say, you'd choose the doctor with two decades of surgeries under her belt. In what are perhaps more relatable terms, would you rather entrust a loan to somebody with a 700 credit score, or a person who can't hold a job for longer than a month and keeps getting evicted? Likewise, would you rather get a loan from an accredited bank or a fast-cash lender? Would you want to be in a committed relationship with a well-known cheater, or someone who has a reputation of treating their partners and others with respect?

Credibility is absolutely essential for the building of trust, be it between yourself or your company and the public, your company and potential investors and business associates, or between yourself and a potential romantic partner. The same goes for determining whether a business, figure of authority, or person is worthy of *your* trust.

When it comes to authoritative and public trust, credibility is everything. In more personal terms, credibility extends from one's "track record," so to speak, and as such, this public perception extends to the lower levels of the pyramid. When it comes to building initial authority, credibility is crucial. One cannot become a celebrity in any sense if nobody knows who they are, an influencer can't influence anyone if nobody believes them, a politician can't politick if no one trusts them, and an expert cannot be considered an expert if they have no credentials. The same goes for if any of these categories of authority are caught in a lie or act of hypocrisy. The potential result is that their credibility collapses, along with their celebrity position and level of trust in the public eye. It might be said that public trust is the most difficult trust to repair.

When it comes to business or professional trust, this level of credibility is slightly more personal. What's more, it is often oriented towards finances, or a financial track record. When asking a bank for a business loan, whether you're a loyal friend and companion, or whether you succeeded in your education makes no difference. What *is* important is how you handled past loans. What matters is if you made all payments in a timely and organized fashion, and if you made a full return on all financial promises. If you have a poor track record, it can be a lot like having a felony on your personal record. You can't take out a loan, you can't rent property in certain areas, you can't find employment in many places, and the list of ways it can thwart you in life goes on and on. Then, as the leader of a company, if you're lacking credibility, it makes people, including potential consumers, investors, or partners, want to avoid conducting business with you. It can be said that credibility is essential to every aspect of building professional relationships between people and businesses.

As one may guess, interpersonal relationships are perhaps the most personal of all, and impacts us on a more emotionally-based level. While financial credibility can be influenced by a past track record, the building of interpersonal relationships is determined by an *emotional action* track record. This track record is determined by actions towards those who were willing to give you that initial chance. Likewise, it's important for *you* to give others that chance to prove themselves worthy of trust or to fail. Then when they do so, you make a point to blacklist them from taking out another "emotional loan," let's say. When building interpersonal relationships, it may be helpful to ask: does this person return favors? Do they have a history of betrayal? Can they be trusted with intimate emotions? The answers to these questions can contribute to their emotional credibility.

It is also important to note that credibility, like trust itself, is something that can be lost far more easily than gained, and the loss of credibility itself cannot be easily washed away. The same would, of course, apply to the lower, and more personal levels of the pyramid. No matter who we are, on some level or another, it is important to consider the fact that our actions bear real-world consequences that will either help or hinder credibility, and thus any future ability to build trust.

Compassion

It is important to be compassionate at all times, showing the person you're trying to build trust with that they matter. You must be empathetic, and able to keep this person, their emotions and values, as well as their wants and needs in mind. Being harsh and blunt towards them might be what they need, but then again it might only be what you think they need from your own perspective. Try and place yourself in their shoes and try to see where they're coming from and how they might be feeling, otherwise you cannot hope to show compassion in a progressive way that will lead to forming a bond of trust.

According to a study conducted in 2006, establishing a policy of compassion in a professional setting lowers stress levels, and bolsters confidence and job satisfaction (Frost 2006). More importantly, it makes people feel cherished, as if they are part of a family. There are a number of ways to show compassion in a professional environment. Practice strong communication, such as paying attention while engaging with someone, maintaining eye contact, and not getting distracted. Encourage others with affirming words, don't hesitate to let someone know when they're doing a good job and that they're appreciated. Check in on your workmates every so often, and be willing to lend an ear if they're having a hard time, maybe even giving assistance to alleviate their workload. Last but not least, show compassion in your word choice. There's nothing wrong with a stern critique, people don't improve their performance if they don't know where the slack is. That said, don't be the Gordon Ramsey of your workplace - no one wants to be treated like an "idiot sandwich," as he would say. Be careful about your tone and word choice when making critiques, making your best efforts not to hurt feelings or offend (Go to Independence University 10 Ways To Show Compassion n.d).

As for relationships in the personal sphere, showing compassion is especially vital for building trust. This means showing empathy, and placing yourself in the other person's shoes. Take into consideration that A: the other person might not have the same emotional requisites as you, and B: nobody is perfect, and part of having a relationship with someone is showing that you're willing to accept those flaws. Being compassionate also means that you make the effort to communicate how you're feeling in an unharmful way, and be consistent about showing the other person that you care. Compassion is something that needs to be thoroughly integrated with the next two components of facilitating trust.

Communication

One of the most important conditions for building a relationship is being communicative with the person with whom you're trying to form a bond. You have to be honest and forthcoming about values, feelings, wants, and needs.

In running a business, it is necessary to be as transparent as possible in a professional sense. Do not withhold important information from your team. If there's something that affects you, odds are that it will affect everyone affiliated with your brand. Next thing is that you need to be honest about who you are. There's nothing wrong with having a certain sense of decorum when you're conducting business with those you aren't on a first name basis with. However, when it comes to being a leader, you have to allow yourself and your true values to shine through when you communicate. People tend not to show interest in following someone who isn't authentic, so you can't be a good leader if you're hiding behind the monotonous mask of the corporate drone.

Strong listening skills are also key. Take the time consistently, on a daily basis and when giving critique, to allow those you're conversing with to voice their opinions and concerns. Be compassionate, engaging, show an interest in what they are saying, and give them sufficient time to say what they need to. Doing so cultivates not only trust, but also respect.

Then when you are the one doing the speaking, be direct and to the point, don't overload the listener with unnecessary information, and again, choose your words wisely as not to offend the listener. Be brief, and dedicate the majority of the allotted time to give a voice to the person you're talking to.

From here, follow through with correlating action. When you say that you're going to address the concerns of your affiliates, you don't need to have a contract or a handshake to make it binding. Your word is your bond, and if you fail to follow through you risk losing your trust, along with your integrity and respect as a leader (CCL 2021).

Having effective communication skills in a personal relationship is not terribly different from a professional relationship in terms of being open, honest, and authentic, as well as doing so with compassion and consistency. It is also similar in terms of the end result of being consistently communicative, in that it establishes trust and a sense of mutual respect. Set time aside to have open discussion with your friend or significant other with whom you're trying to establish trust. Schedule that time if need be, but silently bottling those emotions, needs, and concerns can only do harm when they inevitably come to light.

When the time comes for these discussions, be forthcoming and authentic in these talks, while maintaining an overall tone of thoughtful calmness and compassion. This means being thoughtful and empathetic of your partner at all times. In order to do so, you have to place yourself in the other person's shoes, not only by recognising that each of your needs for receiving affection might be different, but also allowing them the proper time to voice their needs and concerns without interjection. You can begin these talks with questions that are solicitous, benevolent, and open-ended. Begin with considerate pleasantries like asking how their day was. Allow them to vent about their daily tribulations, and with any hope, their anxieties will not be carried over into the rest of the conversation. Then move into the deeper questions:

"how are you feeling? What's on your mind? Do you wanna talk? *Can* we talk about something?" Note that if they aren't receptive, don't press them about it. Part of showing empathy is allowing the other person the patience they need.

Think of the back and forth in these discussions as a proverbial talking-stick: whoever's holding the talking-stick gets to speak without interruption. When it's your partner's turn to speak, listen 80 percent and talk 20 percent. What the other person says might not always be pleasant, but in a thoughtful discussion you have to trust that they wouldn't say it if they didn't think they needed to. In doing so, you are showing respect for that person as well as their opinions and emotions.

If you giving them this opportunity ends with you not being able to hold that talking-stick before the discussion is concluded, this might be something worth briefly interjecting. A relationship and the discussions therein are a two-way street, so don't think that your opinion isn't worth giving voice to as well. It's just as vital to be honest about your needs and values as it is for your partner to.

CONSISTENCY

As you may have noticed from our recurrent mentioning of the term, consistency is the glue that holds all the other conditions together. A significant part of consistency is commitment. Making commitments is paramount to establishing yourself as a trustworthy person, whether you're building a business partnership or romantic relationship. After making these commitments, you have to adhere to them in a timely manner, and you have to do so consistently. Putting forth a consistent effort may not always be easy to adhere to, but it is crucial to the longevity and strength of each relationship. You have to show an ability to repeatedly meet obligations without fail, demonstrating the ability to adhere to promises made. This includes following through with promises made, and showing up at your agreed upon time. In the words of the great philosopher Aristotle, "we are what we repeatedly do. Excellence, then, is not an act, but a habit."

Professionally, you have to be consistent in every aspect. As previously noted, someone can consistently do good work, but if they habitually show up late and shift appointments, they can hardly be considered dependable. If you can't show customers, investors, and partners that you're dependable, this reflects poorly on you as well as your brand, regardless of the quality of your product. As such, trust in you and your brand will falter, and credibility will be lost. In 2013, Business Insider ran a story on Yahoo! CEO Marissa Mayer, who was ousted for her undependability. According to anonymous Yahoo! employees and the executives of the company, Mayer was often late to meetings with them as well as their clients, sometimes by minutes, sometimes by hours. In some instances, she blew off appointments with high-priority clients entirely (Carlson 2013). Along with other poor management decisions, she gained notoriety with the professional community and was turned on by Yahoo!'s clients and stockholders. A year after this story ran, Mayer was ranked number 6 on *Fortune's* 40 under 40, and in 2016, made the list for the worst corporate leaders in the world. The worth of Yahoo!'s stock nose-dived, and the following year, she resigned as CEO.

Mayer disappointed a lot of people with her poor attendance, and even further because of her insistence on the triviality of the matter. She wasn't dependable, nor was she consistent, and as a result, her credibility and people's trust for her suffered immensely. On the bright side, Mayer serves as a prime example of the detrimental consequences of being inconsistent in the professional sphere, and that even CEOs are not exempt. What's more, she is also an example of the fact that even in the worst case of losing public trust, you can always pick yourself up by your bootstraps, which she has shown through her new company Sunshine, a company that specializes in A.I. that she started with a former colleague.

In the personal sphere, inconsistency can be equally as fatal to a person's relationships. Being consistent in a relationship is also a matter of dependability. You have to be there for one another: staying in good contact, unfaltering compassion, spending time together, and being there when you agree to be or when the other person needs you most - these are all marks of a relationship that is consistent. Those in such a relationship are able to fall into a comfortable routine with one another, never doubting that one partner will always be there for the other and vice versa, thereby cultivating assurance and trust. Then there's a relationship that's inconsistent: showing up late or not at all at agreed upon times, flaking out when your partner needs you, failure to communicate, not showing compassion because of mood or circumstance. Inconsistency can even manifest in the form of betrayal or infidelity - inconsistency towards loyalty. If you're thinking this sounds like an emotionally abusive relationship, you'd be right. An inconsistent relationship is a negative relationship, which causes a perpetual state of fight or flight in the suffering party, a constant feeling of fear and uncertainty of when their partner will turn on them or let them down next. This kind of relationship is psychologically dangerous, and isn't built to last unless significant changes are made.

You can think of the five conditions like cement, the foundation for all modern structures. To create cement, you need more than just limestone. It is composed of more than one compound which, along with water, are vital for making structural foundations. Without it, we couldn't hope to build such strong buildings. The same goes with creating a foundation for trust. Without these vital components, trust cannot be established, and our pyramid will be doomed to crumble. With this, we have the conditions to build the foundation of our pyramid.

Now, we are ready to embark upon the first component of this foundation, self-trust. You can attempt to build trust without self-trust, but this structure will be as one built on a foundation of sand, while trust constructed with the foundation will be as a structure built on rock. From this, we should come to understand the importance of improving how we see ourselves and those in our lives who hold the potential of making us into better professionals, better leaders, and better people. The result should give us an improved capacity for strengthening trust in our relationships, both personally and professionally.

2

SELF-TRUST

THE MOST IMPORTANT COMPONENT OF THE FOUNDATION

Everyone has a self-image. That self-image is tied to identity, or more specifically, how we perceive ourselves. This concept is examined in *Psycho-Cybernetics*, by Dr. Maxwell Maltz and became the basis for many personal development experts, like Zig Ziglar and Tony Robbins. At its heart, *Psycho-Cybernetics* deals with the "mind-body connection," which is at the foundation for attaining personal goals. Maltz helped several of his patients create a new relationship with their perception of surgery by advising them to visualize a positive outcome. Creating a positive belief, he discovered, helped the patients establish a better relationship with their bodies, and thus, the prospect of surgery. In this example, a positive inner foundation, or thought, led to a positive physical outcome (Maltz 1967). Dr. Maltzas has helped many people realize their goals, as studies have actually shown that people who are able to mentally visualize that they are capable of losing weight are actually able to do so five times more than those who were only verbally motivated to do so (Solbrig 2018). From weight loss and conquering fears to quitting bad habits and achieving monetary goals, Maltz' theory is about convincing the subconscious that you are capable of making improvements in your life.

"Am I capable of changing my eating habits and losing weight?" "am I capable of not smoking anymore?" The way in which we answer these inner questions determines our self image and, more importantly, whether or not we trust ourselves. If we don't think we're capable of making the necessary improvements in our lives or achieving our goals, this reflects a poor image of self, and that we don't trust ourselves to be capable. Likewise, if we trust ourselves to do so, this is a reflection of a positive self image.

What if this same principle were to be applied to how we build relationships? In this case, the question would be "am I capable of making the changes necessary to be a better leader, partner, spouse, friend, or parent?" You might also ask yourself "am I content with the decisions that I've made in my relationships up to this point? Would I be at peace with my choice of people who I've chosen to surround myself with, and free of all regret if I were to die in the next three months?" If the answer to all these questions is yes, it shows that you are able to trust yourself, and more importantly that you see yourself as someone who is capable and worthy of giving and receiving trust from others. If the answer is no, it means you don't trust yourself, and that you're beating yourself up over past regrets. Confidence that you have and are able to make the right choices in building relationships with others is the foundation for all other forms of trust, and thus the foundation of the pyramid of trust. The fact of the matter is: you can't *expect* others to trust you, nor can you expect to trust others, if you can't even trust yourself.

This is not to say that people are incapable of trusting you if you don't trust yourself, nor are you unable to trust others.

THE PYRAMID OF TRUST

It's the same concept as when people say that you can't expect others to love you when you can't love yourself. It is a cliché, and one that's blatantly untrue to boot. People may perfectly well be able to trust you, and vice versa, even if you don't trust yourself. Some will happily trust you as you are, some may be convinced to trust you regardless, but in the words of Bob Marley, "you can't fool all the people all the time." In other words, you can't *expect* people to trust you when you don't trust yourself. Why is this you may ask? Because when you don't trust yourself, it shows - and quite transparently at that.

When you have poor self-trust, you find yourself in a constant state of anxiety when the time comes to make important decisions. You immediately assume that "I can't" attitude, and from this, you develop a tendency to make "I can't" decisions that are ultimately self-sabotaging, even in the face of knowing fully well what the right decision is. This is an extension of our inner-child, the part of us that spent the entirety of it's early life being told that it has to do the right thing simply because it's the right thing to do. In our adult lives, there's a part of our mind that says "this is the right thing to do and I need to do it. I need to show up to that meeting on time, I need to drop the video games to go support my significant other, I need to show this person that I'm someone that they can depend on for the sake of my credibility and securing my future." In response to this, there's another part of our mind that rejects this notion, saying "why do you need to do any of this? Why do any of these people matter?" It's the part of our brain that convinces us that we're in the right for making decisions that undermine our credibility and dependability with others, and that demonizes those people for having those expectations, or retaliating in some way when we don't live up to them (Shallard 2019). This is what is called the actor-observer bias, and it's what allows us to justify our self-sabotaging actions in the moment, which thereby gives way to deepening the regret and feelings of distrust for ourselves that brought us to make those decisions in the first place. On top of this, those with low self-trust tend to dwell on past failures, building that anxiety and self-doubt even further, while forgetting successes and the actions that lead to the wins as well as the losses (Manson 2021). It's a perpetual cycle that keeps us mired in distrust and misery.

Hence, it's difficult for people to trust you when you don't trust yourself because your lack of self-trust is evident when you commit to self-serving actions that negatively impact those around you. Then when the time comes to atone for said actions by loss of credibility, we often downplay the impact of those actions and demonize the other person, ergo why it's difficult to trust others.

To build self-trust and break out of this vicious cycle, and one must face the self-destructive thoughts and actions spurred by the inner-child with our inner-adult, within whom the right course of action always resides. It starts with recognizing how making the wrong choice might impact those around you, and giving voice to that inner-adult, if only a little. If you can even place a small amount of faith into your voice of reason, you can begin building it up from there while illuminating why the right choice is the right choice as you go, giving yourself insight on what you need to do, why you need to do it, and why you need to trust yourself to make that choice.

To quote Joseph Rudyard Kipling, "trust yourself when all men doubt you, but make allowance for their doubting too." If those around you say you should work your brains out and only be focused on your current job for the next 10 years, what do you do if you want more? What if your internal voice says that you're better than this? Why would you settle for a single track when life is a super-highway of opportunity?

We often have the answers somewhere within ourselves, so when the idea begins to make sense and a plan formulates, trust yourself to put that plan into action and make a decision. A crucial part of building self-trust is the ability to trust that inner voice, instead of allowing the voices of others to cloud your judgment and determine the course of your life and career. You must give the idea the time and space that it needs to grow and process in your mind. It's like play-doh, you need freedom to explore things in your mind. Try activities that give you both the time and solitude needed to contemplate. Try quiet pastimes that give you the chance to think, such as fishing or hiking. Use this time to go on autopilot and think about what plans for the future you can come up with.

Trusting yourself to make important life decisions is the pinnacle of self-trust. From here, you can build and lend the trust you need to others, building relationships, trusting yourself to make the right decisions as they come along, and making your plans come to fruition. Decision making is a part of trust because you're trying to decide what decision to make, and you have to trust yourself to consider hundreds and thousands of different options and to make the best one among all other alternatives.

There's a lot of noise in the world. Between the media and peers trying to give you their version of what's "right" and the most optimal way to be successful, there is hardly a moment of respite for us to think for ourselves. As such, having people around you that can help you realize and tap into the intuition of your inner voice is incredibly important. People who are the same wavelength as you and mirror back your inner voice and help you decipher whether the situation you're in is a mental exploration, or a phase of a relationship that's not fully realized. At times, the right friend that's there to help you explore those things in a safe environment could make all the difference, as they remind you of who you are and who they remember you to be.

In order to build self-trust, one must develop and initiate proactive plans for self-improvement or lifestyle changes. For instance, you may commit to wake up earlier, exercising every day, and quitting your smoking habit. You know what you need to do, and it's on you to do it. If you can trust yourself to follow through on goals that you set for yourself, you can eventually come to trust yourself to adhere to your values and morals, and not betray them. Through this process, you are building self-trust.

Another way to build self-trust is by observing self-trust in others and seeing how they build and maintain their confidence. Find inspiration, not comparison, through nonjudgmental, careful observation of the world and the people around you. Look at your friends and family. How do you see them trying to build trust in themselves? How is it reflected in their relationship with you and those around them? What differentiation does it have with your method, what parts are worth adopting, and what parts don't seem to work? Unfortunately you can't read their thoughts, so consider what their inner voice might be saying and to what degree they trust their own intuition in correlation with their actions.

Acknowledge the ways in which you distrust others throughout your life. Many times, our inability to trust ourselves is deeply rooted in a history of the inability to trust others. Recognizing such patterns is an important way to "unlearn" distrust in ourselves.

First, consider how you might have learned distrust in your adolescence. How did your family treat you? What about friends and peers? How might a past love interest have affected your ability to trust? If you are to find a way to trust yourself by moving past previous trauma, you can't simply brush this aside. Dig deep, consider how accruing distrust in others might be affecting your ability to trust yourself and build present relationships. Then give yourself the time to analyse this, come to terms, and heal. The past is gone, so focus on being in the present with consideration for the future. That said, there is one thing that the past is useful for. Use it to reflect on the times when you trusted yourself. Ask yourself: what sorts of barriers did you have to overcome in order to get there? Learning the times in which you've successfully trusted in and was confident in yourself is instrumental. Take those lessons learned and use them as reference moving forward.

Honor your innate talents and aptitude. What are you really good at? What did you do to develop these strengths or skills? You already have unique talents and abilities, and it's great to validate and recognize them. Validation and self-affirmation can serve as reminders that you are capable and trustworthy.

Identify destructive or unhealthy ways of thinking that serve as cognitive barriers to you believing and trusting in yourself. Your thoughts directly affect your emotions and your emotions affect your thoughts. Learn to tune into your inner voice and recognize when this descends into negative self-talk. Confidence and self-trust requires mindfulness and balance.

Be mindful of how trust is oftentimes built during small, intentional moments. Believing and trusting in yourself is a lot harder to do if you're unclear on your own boundaries, limits, and expectations. Start with naming your own boundaries, values, limits and expectations for yourself. From here, make a point to continue keeping them in the back of your mind, and recognizing the moments where they will be tested and what you need to do to adhere to them.

SOME SELF-TRUST AFFIRMATIONS TO PRACTICE

I am safe, worthy, and valuable.

It's perfectly OK to feel uncertain and doubt myself at times.

In times of uncertainty, my value does not change.

I don't need to have all the answers to everything to trust in myself.

Learning to develop self-trust is a process that takes intention, time, and practice.

I trust and believe in myself to show up purposefully and thoughtfully.

I have many unique abilities and talents, and I recognize and honor them.

Confidence isn't a prerequisite to achieve success.

I know and am clear on my own boundaries and limits, and I live by them.

It is certainly possible to break your own self-trust, just like with any other kind of trust, but likewise, you can build it back up again by using the four conditions of trust. This means consistency in your efforts, self-directed compassion, internal communication, self-honesty, and acting efficiently and competently. We're only human, and we all make mistakes and betray our trust in ourselves. The trick is to realize this fact and be able to move on without getting mired in self-loathing and regret. It's these mistakes and the regret that comes with them that drives us to grow as people. Consider your mistakes and instances of self-betrayal, and use them as lessons that will deter you from ever repeating negative actions again. Live in the present rather than dwelling on the past or being fearful of the future. Keep moving forward, one day at a time, then repeat with each new day.

3
THE TOP OF THE PYRAMID - BLIND TRUST

The top level of our pyramid is blind trust. This level is primarily designated for people who are in leadership roles, like music conductors, coaches, military generals, and similar positions of this nature, along with the associated groups that follow commands. This also applies to the more radical form of blind trust, cultism. This trust is blind because it is predicated on a total suspension of reason in all action, even in the face of risk. In doing so, the people who follow those in the position of leadership become inhuman, cogs that are all working together in a grand cooperative machine, the leader of the group being the propellant, the engine so to speak.

One may blindly follow someone or that person's ideal because of a high level of credibility, and thus, high trust. This might be attained through a position of power one holds. In positions of power or leadership, there needs to be a certain suspension of reason and disbelief. This means putting any reason or logic that might give pause aside, that we may give our undivided trust. To a degree, there needs to be a level of trust that is absolute, that a music conductor will lead the orchestra to perfection, a military commander will lead their troops to victory, a manager will direct their employees in a productive manner. When examining cults and cult leaders, leadership and power may be derived from a suspension of disbelief among followers based on levels of charisma and manipulation rather than actual credentials. Despite potentially complicated power dynamics, your conductor or commanding officer is just your boss, while a cult leader might convince you that being logical and calling it quits is a betrayal of sacred values.

If there is uncertainty, there may be a pause, the "paralysis by analysis" that was previously mentioned at the start of the book. If there is pause for doubt in the grand cooperative mechanism, the entire operation will fall apart - the orchestra will be off key, the football team will lose, the army will fail its mission. In fact, sowing doubt in the ranks of an enemy army has always been one of the most sure ways to win a war.

Let's take a look at some examples of what happens when blind faith in someone takes a turn for the worse - two business leaders that commanded a cult-like level of trust from the public: Elizabeth Holmes and Bernie Madoff.

Elizabeth Holmes, was an American businesswoman who founded the company Real-Time Cures, which in 2003 she renamed Theranos. The company's mission was to revolutionize medical blood tests to become automated, and all that was required was a miniscule amount of blood. Experts claimed that it could not be done, and like Steve Jobs, who she strived to emulate to the point that she often donned the Jobs-stye black turtleneck, she set out to prove the naysayers wrong. It appeared that Holmes was successful in her venture, producing such products as "the nanotube" and the "Edison." The company partnered with Walgreens, and by 2014 Theranos was worth $9 billion, propelling Holmes to the *Forbes* 400. By the end of the next year, there were numerous medical agencies that were using her patented products. However the difference between Elizabeth Holmes and the man she desired to emulate, was that Steve Jobs was actually the technological genius that he claimed to be, while Holmes was no more than a fraud. In 2015, the newly built medical technology empire began to crumble when the Wall Street Journal called BS on the Edison product, thereby launching a thorough investigation of Theranos. On top of this, in 2016 CMS uncovered numerous issues with the Theranos products, and sent a letter of warning to the company as a result. Elizabeth Holmes ran from media source to media source to stomp out these allegations and offer her false reassurance of the integrity of her products. Then came the onslaught of litigations and lawsuits against Theranos, all of which were monetarily settled by Holmes. One of which was by the United States Securities and Exchange Commission in 2018, claiming that Holmes was lying about the income which Theranos was generating, as well as the fact that they were claiming that their products were being used by the U.S. military. Again, this case was settled, in exchange for half a million and 10 years of Holmes' voting rights on the company board. At the end of that same year, most of Theranos employees were laid off, and the company was extinguished and liquidised to the creditors. Holmes now stands to be convicted of defrauding patients and investors and conspiracy, in a court case that is set to begin at the end of August this year. If found guilty, she could potentially be facing 20 years along with a boatload of payments for fines and reparations.

Let's look at another example. If you were anywhere near a news broadcast around 2008, you've probably heard the name: Bernie Madoff. Once considered a financial genius who could defy the will of the stock market, Madoff was amongst the most monumental scandals on Wall Street. He was the founder of Bernard L. Madoff Investment Securities LLC, worth more than $65 billion in investor accounts. He, along with his brother, essentially developed the electronic stock exchange, and became respected advisors of the SEC, acting as the middlemen between stock buyers and stock sellers. His investors, clients, and associates trusted him implicitly. Behind closed doors however, he was reinvesting new investment into old investors, allowing him to produce double-digit stock prices for his clients even during economic downturns - in other words, a ponzi scheme. All of these exchange accounts were fabricated. In fact, Madoff had been pocketing the investments, building a false reputation for his firm and an extremely lavish lifestyle for himself and his wife simultaneously. The FBI and federal prosecutors had been told of the sham after it was reported by a lawyer present when he admitted his crimes to his sons, and when two federal agents arrived on the doorstep of his $7 million Manhattan penthouse in December of 2008, he confessed to everything. Perhaps he had a change of heart, his conscience weighed down from pilfering investors since the 60's. In the end, more than 15,400 claims were filed against Madoff, and the struggle to recover the stolen funds remains an ongoing effort to this day. Madoff was given 10 life-sentences, and died alone in prison earlier this year (Balsamo, 2021).

Another more basic form of blind trust is religion. To believe in something that is neither objective or fathomable, one must have faith and trust in their belief system, and above all others at that. To give complete faith, there has to be complete trust, and from this, a suspension of reason and the need for concrete evidence. Granted, there isn't always a *complete* suspension of logic in this case, save radical sects for example, however there is the suspension of some, which is why this kind of trust should be mentioned in the section concerning blind trust. There could hardly be any better example of taking a leap of faith than religious faith. It is as beautiful as it is subjective.

An interesting aspect of blind trust is that it can overlap with the other levels. This manner of trust makes sense for a position of leadership that requires managing or controlling a group of people in unison, however when it is applied to the lower levels, this suspension of logic can be dangerous when placed in the wrong hands, and can be a hindrance for both the trustor and trustee.

Some celebrities are certainly not beyond commanding a degree of absolute trust, and the same goes with experts, political leaders, and influencers. Like those who command complete trust, authority figures can fail when their trust is thwarted. Ultimately, this results in their career being greatly damaged, if not destroyed entirely.

In regards to the professional sphere, when absolute trust is factored in, this results in what is what is known as a "bad investment." In the world of business, a bad investment can make or break a company, so in this regard, taking a leap of faith is far from the best course of action. If an investor really, trully, believes in the investee, then perhaps it is not as much of a leap of faith as one might believe, there must be some degree of reasoning as to why. Suffice it to say that complete suspension of logic is the worst thing anyone could do for their business.

When it comes to interpersonal relationships, trust is everything, but blind and absolute trust can be extremely dangerous. One partner might end up ignoring red flags while the other might take advantage of their naivete, leading to a toxic and highly volatile relationship. There should always be a level of caution, especially in regards to the personal sphere, such as dedicating your life and self to another person.

Overall, this kind of trust is powerful. It is the kind of trust that can develop civilizations, win wars, and inspire religious faith. It can also be dangerous and regressive in the wrong hands, inspiring people to commit heinous acts in the name of their faith throughout history. The question is, is this kind of faith that suspends logic and human intellect worth the potential destructive outcome? Though it may create a chorus of beautiful music or win games and wars, is this worth the possibility of inflicting ruin and pain upon those involved? I suppose that remains to be seen, though it seems that it hardly ever hurts to have some modicum of logic and caution, especially when approaching life's more personal spheres.

4

THE SECOND LEVEL - AUTHORITATIVE TRUST

A PRELUDE ON PUBLIC TRUST

In case it has not already been surmised from the opening discourse, the term "authority" in this case, does not refer to the law or law enforcement, otherwise known as "authoritarianism." Rather, "authority" is taken to mean *authorities* on certain subjects. We see them all around us from the moment we wake up, in movies, news, social media, magazines, research, and the list goes on.

Celebrities may be authorities on acting, music, the arts, or other mediums. Politicians could be considered authorities on legislation, processes of government, and other matters of state. Influencers are authorities on social media, content, and mass communication methods that spread trends across multiple platforms. Experts are authorities on specific studies and subjects, who are validated through education and/or experience. What all these authorities have in common is that their authority directly correlated with their *credibility*, or public trust. Be it through fame or credentials, the trust of the public entirely determines what an authority's word is worth. What's more, to become an authority on a subject is to understand and speak the language of your intended audience.

How does one rise to becoming an authoritative figure? Public trust doesn't just fall into someone's lap after all... or does it? It can mean a lot of work and consistent results, or just one well-coordinated move to bring your name into the spotlight. Sometimes it is just about the right place, right time, right move, like Nusret Gökçe for example. A chef and butcher from Turkey, Gökçe went from the owner of a chain of mediocre steakhouses to an internet celebrity overnight, being dubbed "Salt Bae" for his debonair application of seasoning in one viral video. One might consider him an authority of sorts, on stylish and theatrical cooking that has drawn politicians and celebrities to his restaurants the world-over. Then again, many people aren't so lucky, and for most becoming an authority figure requires hard work and relentless tenacity.

A great example of someone who worked their way up to becoming an authority is Mark Cuban - CEO, entrepreneur, owner of the Dallas Mavericks, and co-star of the reality TV series *Shark Tank*. Cuban is a self-made billionaire, and his journey to success was by no means an easy one. He was born in Pittsburgh to a working-class family and started working from the age of 12, selling garbage bags, stamps, and coins. Cuban skipped over his senior year of highschool early so he could jump right into getting his bachelor's from Indiana University. He left with nothing but his degree, $60 in his wallet, and a massive student loan debt. After being fired from or quitting three jobs one after the other, Cuban had a realization: he loved technology. He buckled down and taught himself the ropes, and eventually started his own company, MicroSolutions, which he sold to CompuServe for $6 million. In 1995, Cuban along with his business partner and friend Todd Wagner started another company Broadcast.

com, a streaming audio service that they sold to Yahoo for $5.7 billion worth of stock in the company (Lginzy 2017).

So what sets Cuban apart from the rest? What makes him an authority? For those who haven't seen an episode or two of Shark Tank, Mark Cuban's place among the sharks is well deserved. He smells money to be made like a shark can smell blood in the wild. He knows whether a product is going to be profitable or not, and in exchange for part ownership of the company, he can take a growing company and turn it into something truly spectacular. On *Shark Tank* alone, he has made over 100 deals on the show. Aside from thorough media coverage, he's donated to numerous charities like the Fallen Patriot Fund, hosted events and fundraisers, published numerous books, and even offered business advice to companies that were struggling during the height of the COVID pandemic.

Overall, Mark Cuban has covered all of his bases in terms of establishing himself as an authority and building public trust for himself and his brand. This is what it means to build trust as an authority figure and a business leader. You build your public image through painstaking and meticulous PR, and make sure all of your customers, clients, partners, and other associates see you as consistent and dependable. Be patient, follow the 5 C's, be upright, love your work, and success will come. As for having thorough PR, the following chapter will cover all the ins and outs of this aspect, and through this, the building of public trust in you and your brand.

5
THE THIRD LEVEL - BUILDING PROFESSIONAL AND PUBLIC TRUST

Would it be wise to invest in something without a level of certainty in monetary return? Hopefully, the answer to this is no. That is, of course, unless you have some kind of personal attachment, or if you truly believe in the product, or otherwise you're just in the mood for taking a gamble. Investing always involves some variation of risk, there's the chance that you may lose some money in the process, or that you may not get the type of return on your investment (ROI) that you were expecting. However, would you willingly enter into a business relationship where you are potentially handing over thousands of dollars and not trust the person with whom you're conducting business? Again, one would hope that the answer to this question is a no.

It's not very sound practice to frequently take abnormally high risks in investment. A sound business relationship is predicated on trust. Financially speaking, the business must present more than just an opportunity, but a certainty that there will be a return to some degree, otherwise, this would be more a charity than an investment. The point of investing in its truest sense is to locate opportunities that have a high potential for growth, and thus, return.

Certainty is essential to human progress. Any sense of certainty stems from feelings of trust. Especially regarding business agreements, placing one's trust in three components is vital for building certainty: one's self, the information received, and the business credibility of partners. This goes for the investor as well as the potential client or partner. Trust, therefore, is really the most vital factor on both ends of every business deal.

In their 1995 study of trust, "An Integration Model of Organizational Trust," Roger Mayer, James Davis, and David Schoorman define this kind of professional trust as a "willingness of a party to be vulnerable to the action of another party based on the expectation that the other will perform a particular action important to the trustor, irrespective of the ability to monitor or control that other party." They also propose that the type of trust that goes into business relationships is composed of three components (Mayer, Davis, Schoorman 1995). The first is ability - in other words, the assurance that the person on the other end of the deal is competent. Then comes integrity, or assurance that the other person has a set of moral or ethical guidelines that they will not cross, that they won't pull the rug from under the other person once they have what's theirs, so to speak. The final component is benevolence, not necessarily that they're utterly selfless, but more or less that they just aren't an immoral, money grubbing monster who has no passion for anything about their business except making a quick buck, and no care for who they trample over to get it (though, one might say this just goes back into the integrity section). What these three components have in common is assurance, and thus, trust that the person on the other end of the business deal will conduct themselves in a professional manner. This is determined on the manner in which a person builds their brand and their track record in PR and with their clients. But how does one build their brand name?

When discussing the building of a brand's name, the methods in which to do so deviate between a small business scale and a multi-million dollar company. With regards to building the name of a smaller business, there are still numerous factors to consider. This is namely in the form of building the reputation brand in the public eye, as well as building professional relationships with potential consumers, investors, and partners. Playing a major role in all of these factors, we once again have trust. Making a brand that appeals to as many people as possible is the goal in this regard obviously, but being involved with the public that you're trying to pander to is just as important. This establishes your company's values, competency, and commitment. You're essentially justifying why the public should put its trust in you and your brand above all other competition.

When it comes to building professional relationships at this level, you need to consider personal value - what you're getting out of another person in a professional relationship and what they're getting out of you in return. Building trust in any relationship can sometimes be considered a law of equivalent exchange, and this is especially so in regards to professional relationships. Again, is the other person worthy of trust, investment, or partnership? What is the return? What is their track record with utilization and return of such trust? Likewise, when building public trust for yourself as an investor or your company, how do you do so? It boils down to that track record, the values, competency, and commitment that has been established through your past actions as a leader, and how it reflects on your company. It is not unlike the authority level of trust - in a way, you and your brand are an authority on whatever product you're trying to sell. Credibility on a professional level is just as important as it is for becoming an authority.

THE PYRAMID OF TRUST

Trust may not cover every aspect of building a brand from startup to multi-billion dollar conglomerate, but it is undoubtedly critical to growth. In the business world, trust is relative to how people view your brand, which is something that can make or break any company. How people see your brand is everything because these people are potential customers, investors, promoters and business partners, none of whom are going to get on board with a business that is shoddy, has poor values, and is untrustworthy. If you want people to pay you and facilitate your pathway to success, you need to forge bonds of trust with them, otherwise owning a profitable business will be nothing more than a pipe-dream.

How do you build a track record you may ask? How do you establish a public image for you and your company? As we've said, you have to participate with your intended public and build credibility.

There's more than one way to skin a cat, as the saying goes, and this certainly applies to the matter of building public trust and gaining credibility as a figure of authority. In the modern era, there are numerous ways to improve personal image and credibility. You might recognise some of these from Mark Cuban's method. These techniques include:

Writing a book
Media attention
Social Media Marketing
SEO content
Podcasts
Video content
Events
Charity

Writing a Book

One of the best ways to build public trust in the 21st century is to become an author. To start, you may choose to position yourself as an expert in a given area that you're exceptionally well-versed or talented in. Or, you may choose to write a book that details a problem or issue that people might have and how your brand is the solution to that problem. Then, if you're going to become an author, you might as well become a best-selling one. Currently, there are five major best-seller lists: Amazon, Barnes & Noble, *USA Today*, *Wall Street Journal*, and the *New York Times*.

At the lowest rung is Amazon. Best-selling titles are determined by an hourly algorithm. That means a book's ranking can change on any given hour. It's better than not being a best-seller at all but, it's not necessarily something that's newsworthy for the mainstream media. The media already understands that becoming an Amazon best-seller is not that difficult. As such, gaining credibility and public trust through Amazon's list alone will simply not suffice, though it's a good stepping-stone to continue to get to that point.

Next is Barnes & Noble. Becoming a Barnes & Noble best-seller is a fairly decent accomplishment, though it's very similar to how you would become an Amazon best-seller. Their lists are updated daily rather than hourly, but Amazon and B&N are similar in that they factor the total number of sales for a short period of time. Therefore, you have a better chance of making it to the top of the list on any given day.

More credible than this are the lists published by *USA Today* and *The Wall Street Journal*. Their bestsellers are aggregated weekly, from Sunday to Saturday. So, you'll want to sell as many copies as you can from Sunday to Saturday, and you want these sales to be diversified, meaning the sales are coming from different channels; some from Amazon, some from Barnes & Noble, and some from Kobo, the Walmart bookstore. Of course, there are other online bookstores. Typically, to reach one of these lists, authors or publishers will sell anywhere between 7,000 and 20,000 units within a week timeframe. It really depends on the competitiveness of the week.

To give an example, Authors Unite (Tyler Wagner's company) has actually gotten somebody to the number two spot on *The Wall Street Journal* list in August 2020, and only sold 6,500 copies. However, a book that's selling in one of the top book sales months, like in December or January, those sales number would have to be closer to 10,000 copies to hit these lists.

Finally, often regarded as the "gold standard," is the *New York Times* best-seller list. *The Wall Street Journal* is more geared for business professionals, and being on their best-seller list would be most beneficial for a book written for a correlating audience. Meanwhile, the *New York Times* list is directed to a broader audience of consumers and stakeholders, and perhaps more respected in the publishing world. There's a strategy that goes into making the *New York Times* list. First, you'll need to have your media in line. In other words, you'll want to have some kind of existent and somewhat prominent media presence to begin with. Also, you really want to get published by a traditional publisher. Then, you also want to register physical-copy sales in as many different bookstores as possible. There are actually specific bookstores that the *New York Times* looks at.

A well-developed strategy takes months to years to put together and execute, and you really need to coordinate it properly so all these sales get counted. The strategy to get book sales would rely on the following:

Building an audience through your content, which can be through your website blog, social media channels, writing for large publications and even videos on places like youtube or tiktok) so the followers would be happy to buy your book to consume more of your content.

Getting corporations to buy bulk orders of your books instead of paying for a consulting or speaking fee.

Running paid ads often via Facebook or Amazon for book sales

Having influencers promote the book when they contain your ideal audience by building relationships with them

Utilize affiliates via places like clickbank

Purchasing an email blast from other people's email lists.

On the back end, you have the power of a traditional publisher behind you and verification through other media channels.

Get book endorsements from high profile people

Go on podcasts is one of the most effective strategies to selling books

Speak at local libraries and bookstores like barnes and noble

As you can probably imagine, it's a lot easier to establish public trust when you're sitting higher up in the hierarchy of the trust. A celebrity or authority is going to have an easier time getting people to buy from them or trust them than someone who is unknown. Why would you take advice on growing income and becoming a millionaire from somebody who is barely making payroll? Most likely not.

One of the best ways to establish trust in the 21st century is to be verified on social media. That blue check mark you see on people's Instagram, Facebook or Twitter profiles basically means they are someone important, including a renowned expert, celebrity, musician, politician, influencer, or any other influential public figure.

THE PYRAMID OF TRUST

So, if you make the *New York Times* or *Wall Street Journal* best-seller lists, you're going to gain credentials, be in the news, and gain a lot of media attention, if only for a moment. This is going to make the case to help you in becoming verified, but this alone won't be enough to succeed in achieving the verification you need. To get in the *New York Times*, you're going to need as much media attention as possible, across multiple platforms.

What's really going to help when people google you is Wikipedia, which is also a very powerful way to help you achieve verification on many media platforms. Though, you're going to need legitimate media to get a page on the website. If you're successful in acquiring one, it will prove quite useful in earning renown and public trust. In a way, it's like a brief and easily accessible biography that's available to anyone, free of charge. What's more, having real, tangible credentials and media coverage is going to help you get a Wikipedia page that won't be deleted. However, this is a somewhat minor mark of public trust and credibility. The remainder of this chapter will detail more vital forms of media and public participation for building the repute and public trust of one's brand.

Media Attention

Bill Gates famously said that even if he were down to his last dollar, he would invest everything he had left in PR because that's where you control the perception around you. The key is to focus on the delivery of your brand and being mindful that the language you use determines how others will perceive you. We cannot stress enough the importance of good PR. If you can get media recognition, this will also help your SEO, as well as the name of your brand overall. Even when your brand finally advances to something truly profitable, the importance of maintaining this public image will remain.

One of the best ways, aside from writing a book, for increasing one's name recognition is through public relations, and the most widely trusted form of PR is going to be TV interviews. To get yourself on TV, you need to either hire a PR firm, or know who to pitch with a powerful story that will align with the interests of a particular network or program. Do your research on what a show is looking for and how it works, and then find the contact information of the producer which can be done via Linkedin, Instagram, a website with an email finding tool like hunter.io, and so forth. The best way to build a story is something that we can borrow from Hollywood movie production, which is the three act structure. This is the setup (who are we targeting), the conflict (their struggle), and the Resolution (the solution to the struggle). Then the most important part is how you are the "Bridge," meaning how you are going to help them connect the dots between the conflict they are struggling with and the resolution they desire. Now that we have this, we are going to build a powerful pitch, using the following formula. Find a timely news hook relevant to the outlet, focus on the topic first and then figure out how to strategically position yourself, and bolster your claims with facts, stats and figures. From this, put together 3-4 talking points and ask them if they would be open to having you on the show.

Another pro tip is to focus on local tv stations first, especially if you were born, grew up or currently live there. Eventually you will build a media portfolio, experience and confidence with TV, and from there, you can move up to larger broadcasting stations.

Furthermore, if you're a best-selling author, as compared to an unknown, it's going to be a lot easier to get TV interviews. Don't forget to write that book and get as high as you can on the bestseller listings. Improve (or establish) your name recognition and make the connections between your name and a subject area, so that you can cultivate the reputation as an expert in your niche. It will open the doors for everything else that you do.

Once you establish yourself as an expert with a book, the next step is to go for another form of media, such as placement in online publications like Forbes, which has over 50+ million visits a months. Online publications are a great way to get exposure and credibility for your brand and are often easier to get featured in than printed magazines, where instead of waiting up to a year for printed, this can be done within 48 hours or upto 12 weeks. When we are talking about getting placements in online publications, we need to understand the different types of articles available.

The most valuable form of online publication exposure is to be a contributor to publications, also known as authorship. This allows you to build up thought leadership, and cannot be bought by PR agencies doing outreach. When you are a contributor, people will see the work you have published and reach out to connect with you for opportunities to be featured in your upcoming articles. This also enables you to reach out to people to connect with them to learn and tap into their expertise, whilst "sourcing information" as a writer.

The second most valuable form of online media exposure for most people is known as a full feature, where an editor or contributor writes an article about you or your company, which helps tremendously in obtaining the blue checkmark verification status on social platforms like Instagram. The downside to these full features is that often these articles don't perform as well in terms of traffic, unless you are a big brand or name like Apple or the Kardashians. Another great way to get in the media is to get yourself quoted as an expert amongst other experts, known as a feature or mention for a topic, which often will get way more traffic. The last form of online media attention has become tougher, but when being featured in a listicle with a bunch of experts like our co-authors Aimee &

Imran, who were featured as Top 20 Entrepreneurs in Forbes, can be powerful and help open a lot of doors.

If you're willing to dedicate a good chunk of time on cold outreach to get in the media, there are a few ways to approach this. The key is to start smaller and build credibility before going for something like Forbes or Fortune. You could try HARO, but if you go this route, expect to do a lot of work for months and see little results. You may get lucky, but to increase the odds of getting visibility, we recommend that you sign up for the highest package to get first dibs on pitch writing and journalists.

The route we recommend is to hire a PR agency with a solid track record of happy clients and one that is able to actually deliver. There are tons of firms that work on a retainer basis and may charge you anywhere from $5,000 to $30,000 each month. They may present you with a list of media publications that they will pitch for you, with no guarantees that any of these outlets may pick up your story. A lot of people have gotten screwed over by these agencies who promised a lot upfront, but failed to deliver. To avoid wasting thousands of dollars on PR without any measurable output, we highly recommend you working with an agency that offers a money back guarantee if they fail to deliver the a la carte services.

The next form of media that is extremely long and worth a lot is being featured in printed magazines or newspapers. This isn't much different from pitching online publication editors. One of the best ways to stand out for this is to email editors, offering to meet them at the office whilst bringing something interesting to talk about such as unique story ideas. When pitching the publications for print and you don't hear back from them, be sure to also pitch their online publication because the online has infinite space for content, whilst the printed has very limited space. If you do decide to pitch in person, aim to get a meeting with an editor. As a follow-up after the meeting, be sure to send a thank you note with a personalized gift to really stand out.

Podcasts

In recent years, podcasts have become a prevalent medium for communication and outreach. Audio content is trending upwards, and provides an opportunity for people to digest information while they're doing other things. Listenership is also at an all-time high, and it doesn't look like that's going to change anytime soon. This is especially so since COVID has inspired a lot of influencers and celebrities of every calibre to focus on podcasting to retain their fanbases.

Podcasts are a good way to spread your brand name even further, as well as participate with the public. Considering the current high popularity of podcasts, getting your business spoken about by prominent celebrities and influencers that host their own podcasts is a great way to promote and build public trust. Actively participating in podcast interviews as well as offering podcast hosts ad revenue in exchange for shoutouts regarding your company and its products will help you gain traction in this medium.

Co-author Tyler Wagner started a podcast about two-and-a-half years ago. He has now interviewed over 2,000 people, including some really big celebrity, authority-type individuals like Gary Vaynerchuk. Just how did he manage to pull off a meeting with someone like Gary? Tyler was interviewing one woman, and she asked him at the end of the interview who he would like to have on his show. "Who's your dream guest?" she asked, and Tyler said "Gary V." That same day, she sent a screenshot of her asking Mr. Vaynerchuk if he would come onto the show, and he graciously agreed. Within six months, they flew out to meet in person and had their interview. Since Tyler got Gary V on his show, he gets

40-50 pitches a week now. His team vets the pitches and accepts five a week.

Tyler started his podcast for fun because he was at a place with his business where it could operate and scale on its own. He would interview as many people as possible, and some of the interviewees naturally became his clients. Out of every 20 people he interviewed, three of them would become a client. He never pitched them for business, but they approached him after. It happens so naturally because they enjoyed the podcast recording and learned what Tyler specializes in and has to offer.

A lot of successful people love to tell their story. It's a way to connect with powerful people. You'll get some no's, but a lot of yeses. From a networking standpoint, you can grow your network with podcasts to a level where most people aren't aware of.

Having your own podcast allows you to harness a wealth of knowledge. You connect with so many people, and from there, you're able to connect the dots. Tyler started connecting with tons of PR people and was able to put them into a team, thereby creating a PR powerhouse.

To start off, he did short 10-20 minute interviews and reached out to as many people as possible through LinkedIn and Instagram. Then after he did 1,000 interviews, he realized that he was yearning for deeper, more meaningful conversations that you can't have in 20 mins. So he started doing 1-hour long interviews and started vetting people and building mutually beneficial relationships. If you interview someone and they have a large following, you'll promote them and they'll promote you. Be strategic and determine if your goals are aligned. Tyler reached out to a lot of PR people in particular because if he interviews someone in PR, they could get more visibility, and he would give them more visibility. They could join forces in PR, and collaborate through his publishing company, Authors Unite, so it's a 4-way win.

THE PYRAMID OF TRUST

Tyler outsources the content editing and hires a team that helps edit each podcast, which he then shares on Linkedin. One interview can turn into 10 pieces of content, so you could easily post a couple times a week. Doing podcasts is a great way to hack content. If you do a couple interviews a week, you'll always be actively pumping out new content on your social channels.

When people schedule a podcast with Tyler, they book it through his Authors Unite website. Therefore, anyone who schedules a podcast will probably get curious and poke around his website that just so happens to have a Facebook Pixel, which retargets Facebook and Instagram ads about successful client stories. Hence, the podcast guest is aware of their capabilities and expertise before they even come on the show.

Interview as many people as possible to start, get in your flow, and figure out if you like a shorter, medium or longer type of show. Then become highly strategic about it and make sure whoever you interview is aligned with your goals and what you're trying to accomplish. If your goal is to grow your business, then only interview potential partners or clients. For fun conversation and business, then interview people for both. If your goal is to grow your own personal following, then interview people with large followings. It's all about finding out what your ultimate goal is and reverse engineering to achieve that. The more interviews you do, the more knowledge and resources you'll have to grow your relationships and help your clients.

Regardless of your business or profession, a good podcast can help you grow exponentially. Consider starting a podcast if you really want to grow your business and online presence. First, start small. Interview people with a decent media following. They'll share those interviews with that audience, so between that and the interview itself, you will gain credibility. Slowly start to work up to more popular interviewees in correlation with your own popularity and experience. When you yourself have a nice following and some experience with interviews under your belt, move on to interviewing people who have large audiences who will cause your public trust to skyrocket. The interviewees and audience members could even become clients or business partners.

There's tremendous opportunity in building your own podcast, and the best part is, you can accomplish significant growth without spending money on ads. Say you're just starting a business and you don't have a large marketing budget. Producing a podcast is one of the best ways to grow a business without an advertising budget for more traditional forms of outreach. A podcast will also add to search engine results that include your name and brand information. Again, this is essential for expanding an online footprint, brand, and business.

Reviews are also important because they will be viewed as proof that your product or service is worth people's hard-earned money. Assuming reviews are consistent and positive, all this publicity over multiple platforms generates *content*, which is imperative for expanding a brand.

The content you put out is going to tell people about the problems you're solving, and will determine the type of clients and people you're going to attract. As an example, if your content provides methods for earning your first $10,000 in a month, do you think you're going to be attracting people who are already millionaires? Probably not, since what you're saying doesn't really apply to them. To give a less obvious example: say you're writing for a magazine about pets. You're a dog person, and it shows in your writing. However, a statistical analysis of the readers who purchase the magazine show that the audience consists predominantly of cat lovers, by a landslide at that. Would you continue writing dog-oriented pieces for the magazine, if you continue with them at all? If you want your writing to be recognized and accepted by your audience, you would either research your heart out on cats, adopt a cat to get some inkling of an idea as to what you need to write about, or give up with the publication all together.

One of the business associates in Imran's real estate business, Matt Gowdy, has become an expert at "cold calling," meaning that he can quickly establish trust with clients, largely because he has gained knowledge on interpersonal communication. He told me that what we think we're saying and what the other person is hearing are not necessarily the same. It's what they *hear* that's going to determine if they're going to trust you or give you their time and money, which they aren't going to know until the initial exchange has concluded, be it in-person or what they have read from a quick visit to the internet. Language is so important when you design your content, so be sure to keep this fact in mind at all times.

Video content

Video content can be highly effective for expanding a brand and getting you vast exposure. In general, people are more likely to trust a video more than audio or a blog. In-person meetings are the most effective, but this isn't always feasible from a standpoint of time, money, distance etc. With video conferencing, like what you see on YouTube or LinkedIn, you can let thousands of people join in on the conversation; they can feel like they are connected with you through video. That's why Instagram stories and reels became so popular, along with social media features like Instagram Live and Facebook Live. TikTok took off because the platform allows people to communicate through the versatile medium of video. It's for people who consume, engage, and connect with people around the world, even when they're apart.

Shay Rowbottom, a prominent Linkedin influencer and CEO of her own marketing business, amassed some 600,000 followers in less than two years. She wasn't talking about business at the time; people saw her following groups. They saw the impact she was making and the authenticity of it all, and from this, they would like her and connect with her. Because they're connected with everyone else, their audiences merged together as a singular following. Then they paid her to show other people how to get it done. Understanding that a lot of social media networks utilize newsfeeds where you are being discovered vs people actively looking for your content, so make sure to leave a positive user experience, which means you don't have time to introduce yourself as nobody is owing you a view at all, so grab their attention and they can visit your profile afterwards to know more about you. When it comes to making videos, you really need to know your target audience so you can clearly define the following: What is the key takeaway? What thoughts will they have after watching your video? What actions will they want to take?

To also gain attention in the newsfeed, utilize a top bar to tell what the video is going to be about and drive curiosity in a color format to help you stand out on Linkedin.

Don't be afraid to be expressive in your videos! This is key because people may not listen to the audio or read subtitles. The top three lines need to be attention-grabbing. Now, also engage genuinely with everyone who comments. The more engagement you foster and the more often you post, the faster you will grow.

Suffice it to say, visuals matter. By no means do you need a huge budget or an expansive production studio for your videos. Nowadays, an iPhone works just fine. Though on the other hand, you certainly can't pitch your services to a corporation in a dark room, with a shoddy-looking camera that was made a decade ago. If your visuals appear to be poor quality, they may lend reason distrust; therefore, it's imperative to make sure that the visual quality connotes trust.

When recording the video, it is okay to make mistakes. It's rare to make a video without any editing. Doing all of the editing on your own is not a good use of your time, and we strongly advise against it. Hiring someone off Fiverr or Upwork to do the video editing for you could be a total game changer that will make your life so much easier.

Social Media Marketing & Paid Advertising

Two of the most popular platforms right now are Instagram and Tiktok. A lot of people will focus on vanity metrics and try to do many things to create a perception of being an influencer and will buy shoutouts to grow their following of people who aren't legitimate followers.

Content Creator Angie Lee believes that instead of trying to create a large following or the latest hack on each platform, it's best to build a tribe of people and treat each person as a person with a heartbeat. When creating the content, Angie suggests to really focus on the 3P's: person you help, problem you solve, promise you make. The problem you are solving needs to be searchable, specific and solution based.

When creating your bio, treat it like the first impression you are making on someone. With that being said, create content that is savable and share-worthy, as "shares" are worth more than "likes" and helps you achieve greater exposure to new audiences faster.

On Instagram, the reels/stories are tools that are there to help you connect with the audience. Any platform like Instagram, Facebook, etc. allows you to send direct messages and can be used to generate leads and actual sales.

When making content, Angie Lee suggests you always position yourself as a teacher, friend, or thought leader. From a teacher's standpoint, you can use a "how to" educational format. You may also build a connection or tell a story through positioning yourself as a friend. Last but not least, you may choose to position yourself as a thought leader who challenges the status quo, industry norms, and create a shift in perspective.

For Paid Advertising, a great strategy to identify what content and audiences work to build trust and authority is by Dennis Yu, who utilizes the $1/day strategy, which is an easy way to go about testing your content on social media without spending a fortune. To implement this, you simply boost a post over seven days, while adding on new boosted posts every day in tandem.

During your first week, the most you'll spend in a single day is $7. Get rid of 90% of posts that don't perform, then add $30 for an additional 30 days for the posts that do well, and identify the real unicorns through higher budgets and testing new audiences.

"When you first start boosting," Dennis says, "it's going to take a while to find out what combination of factors works best for your campaigns. It's key to document your process and develop what we call 'repeatable excellence'. A good way to do this is by taking notes. Write things down, take screenshots, and create checklists that, when followed, can replicate this tested success. You want your junior folks to do this for you, right? You set the example for others to follow—then delegate yourself out of doing this every day."

Search Engine Brand Results & Search Engine Optimization

To build a public image for you and your brand, you must leverage the power of networking across multiple platforms and Search engine optimization (more commonly known as SEO). Search engine optimization essentially relates to how far up the list you and your brand is on a search engine. The reason we mention search engines vs Google is that Bing has over 33% of all search engine traffic and Yahoo has about 10% of the traffic. The most desirable outcome is that you're the first thing that people see when they enter your name or search for problems that can be solved by your business. To

THE PYRAMID OF TRUST

do this, you must get a high click-rate as you network across multiple platforms, and accumulate large followings across social media platforms, including Facebook, Instagram, Twitter, and more. The more clicks that your pages get, the more likely that they will become the first of the options that appear on a search engine.

Once your name starts to circulate as a result of successful PR work, people will now search on Google or their preferred search engine. When doing so, they're going to look at where you come up in search results. Hence, it's important to consider: how are people going to perceive you when they see you or your company come up on their search engine? Your search results matter for your brand, and your branding is more critical than anything because it determines how people will view your brand identity. You have your self-identity, but your public identity and perception is based on how you present on social media, and where you appear after a quick search on Google, Bing, Yahoo, etc.

To build that brand identity, one may start by publishing a book and getting it on the Amazon list and Barnes & Noble list, which will help build the brand-producing search results. You then get extensive media coverage across every conceivable online medium, and from this, you come up more and more frequently throughout the internet. You have social media pages, you have reviews, you have interviews, and all the while, more and more people are entering your name or the name of your company in that search bar and pressing "Google Search" (or hitting the "Enter" key). Before you know it, you've hit the pinnacle of Google search results and are the first to appear after you hit your respective choice of "search" button.

It's all really a simple matter of S.E.O., or "Search Engine Optimization." Some have built entire companies for the purpose of helping people and their businesses and products come up first on a search engine. The fact of the matter is, many people aren't going to bother going past that first page to search for what they want. This is why the closer you are to the top of that neverending list of search results, the better visibility for you and your company. The truth is, being at the top of people's search results is a badge of credibility on its own.

To do S.E.O, you must understand the fundamentals. With these guidelines, you will be better off than most S.E.O Agencies. Be mindful that Google is trying to provide its users the best search results possible to attract the biggest user base, which allows them to have traffic and data and attract advertisements, which makes up a good percentage of their revenue. In order to achieve this, whilst most people will focus on 200+ algotherims, we advise you to focus on four core ones.

The first is user intent. In order to get users to want to click on your website, you must identify what they're looking for, provide content and solutions to solve this, giving them the information they need to keep coming back. The second part is user experience. Would you want to use a website that is hard to use or is slow to load? Probably not, which leads to the third point on trusted authority. When people go on a website, the first thoughts that come to mind are: Is the brand legitimate? Is the person behind the brand an expert in the field? The fourth is relevance, which ties heavily to user intent, but when considering how to sculpt relevance on a website, the most important is a website title, the description that shows up on Google, and a header that contains your main keywords. With this, the next important thing is to do guest posting on relevant websites and get backlinks to your websites, which is just the hyperlink that is clickable to your website. Remember to focus on providing valuable content to solve people's issues and keeping these four things in mind on your own website or guest posts and you will be good. Even if Google or other search engines have updates, these four will always remain unchanged.

Events

Another good way to build trust is by holding events, hosting or speaking at them to be specific. Events are a great way to establish public trust. One might even say that they represent the formation of trust relationships. Take Secret Knock by Dr. Greg Reid for example. Secret Knock is amongst the top networking events in the world. When you pay to attend the event, you don't know where it's going to be held, except for the city, and the date. You don't know the venue, who the speakers are going to be, or even who's going to be attending. Regardless of uncertainty, the people who attend will pay every single year to attend the event because Reid under-promises and *over*-delivers. One year for example, he brought in Tonino Lamborghini. He also brings in people like Brian Smith, the founder of Ugg Boots, other billionaires, leading experts in their fields like Rob Klein, as well as many A-list celebrities. The guests agree to come with no promise of how many guests are going to be there. They trust that Reid will deliver. As you can probably imagine, the event is sold out every year.

Speaking at events can be huge as well. A strong speech gives you that clout, that sense of power and influence. If people are willing to pay to listen to you speak, that places you very high on the hierarchy of trust. As with speaking at bigger stages, start locally and small. A great example of this is Toastmasters, a nonprofit organization that promotes communication, public speaking, and leadership. After that, make a list of your ideal places to speak with your unique message that would be a fit for these events and build a relationship with them.

Events are a great way to promote public trust in you and, in this case, your brand. You have to be proactive and participate with potential investors and customers, and hosting an event or participating in one as an exhibitor is an exceptional way of doing just that. Obviously live events are the best way to go, as they allow you to interact with potential customers and investors in-person and in a suitable environment. However, hosting online events is also an option, such as streaming workshops or webinars, and while it may not have the same effect of face-to-face interactions, it does give potential customers and investors the chance to learn about your product in a convenient and comfortable manner.

Charity

Donating to charity and holding fundraisers are other productive ways to build trust between your business, potential customers, and investors. Charitable giving associates your brand with good values and compassion, both vital components to establishing trust. Charity is a great way to build the reputation and positive public opinion of your company. So if you're at the stage where your business is thriving and you've got the extra income to expand or as tax write-offs, research a good cause that you align with and begin creating a more positive image for your brand.

A lot of people with full-time jobs choose to volunteer in the nonprofit sector as a means to not only connect with others, but also make an impact. It's also a great way to align with people who share your values. Furthermore, if those people are well-connected themselves, it can be a genuine way to reach higher levels of trust within the sector you are working in.

All of these different methods are important to building image and credibility at the authority level of trust, as well as the following level, professional trust. These methods of accumulating trust should be kept in mind when attempting to build self image and public trust for one's self, as well as for building that of one's company.

6

TAKING CHAPMAN'S FIVE LOVE LANGUAGES TO THE NEXT LEVEL

INTERLUDE TO INTERPERSONAL TRUST

Let's take a look at Nobel Prize winner Daniel Kahneman's work on the correlation between decision making and happiness. He uses economic theories to underlay his theories on happiness rather than economic value creation. Essentially, he connotes that creating economic value, or satisfaction, is different from creating happiness. Happiness is temporary and fleeting, and he says that the best way of generating happiness is spending time with loved ones. On the other hand, satisfaction is more long-lasting, created by achieving personal and professional goals. It is generally associated with building one's economic value. Kahneman notes that focusing on one has the potential of hindering the creation of the other. For example, people who bind themselves to building satisfaction don't have as much time on their hands to spend with loved ones, and as such they are often unable to experience happiness as often as someone who might prioritize this feeling.

The real differentiation is how these experiences are perceived. Accomplishments are a part of our past, and are based on how we spent our lives as a whole, and whether or not it was productive. Happiness is based solely on fleeting feelings experienced only in the present. We often associate accomplishing goals and meeting expectations with the pursuit of happiness, though from Kahneman's theory, we might gather that this may not necessarily be the case - but how does this relate to building trust? One might say that this theory embodies the difference between building professional trust and interpersonal trust. Building economic value is based on accomplishment in the professional sphere, and meeting the expectations of those with whom we are attempting to create trust in a professional relationship with. Contrarily, building trust in interpersonal relationships is geared towards generating and increasing feelings of happiness.

And what affects our happiness and life fulfillment more than our romantic relationships? Lisa Fei, founder of Clarity, the relationship wellness platform saw that the people around her were struggling immensely due to their love life, which was often their greatest plight. After being engaged to a man who was unfaithful, she struggled for years in her love life because she was too busy looking in the rear view mirror. Therefore, Lisa made it her life's mission to empower others with the right tools and resources to thrive in their relationships, which were never given or taught in school.

People have AA and rehab for substance abuse, where they gather together to talk about similar problems and find a solution in their own lives, but where do people turn to for help in their relationships, which are arguably the most important aspects of one's life? This is why Lisa was inspired to build a comprehensive platform that gives people a community to safely and discreetly confide in others who can relate, and brings together over fifty of the world's top dating and relationship experts to help people successfully navigate every aspect of their love journey.

One of the biggest topics explored on Clarity is trust, which is a huge component and the very anchor of every healthy and lasting relationship. It's imperative to have the ability to discern who to trust and who not to trust.

"Relationships are all about trust and respect. It's of the utmost importance to respect the people that you're dating enough to give them the benefit of the doubt and trust. The real question is: why even get involved in a relationship if you go into it with phobias and problems when it comes to trust?" says Lisa.

When you carry the incessant fear of getting hurt because you gave someone your trust and that person somehow lets you down or falls short of delivering, you may take it out on someone who is actually deserving of your trust, and now you stand the chance of hurting them and damaging your relationship. Many people easily give their trust right off the bat to whoever they're dating and fail to assess things clearly when they are in love. They have their rose colored lenses on, and see the signs, yet choose to ignore them, which can lead to suffering and heavy consequences down the line.

Making the decision of who you're going to have a relationship with or spend the rest of your life with is perhaps the most important decision you'll ever make—your life's happiness and fulfillment may depend upon it.

Before cracking open the following chapters on interpersonal trust, it's important to consider this vital and psychologically viable theory in regards to building interpersonal relationships: Dr. Gary Chapman's Love Languages. Whether building trust and closeness between friends or romantic partners, Chapman's love languages theory offers unique insight in regards to building more powerful bonds by stepping outside of ourselves, and taking other people into consideration in a manner that is free of our own perceptions.

According to Dr. Chapman's bestseller from 1992, *The 5 Love Languages*, the theory is more or less about the understanding of how to connect with others in a meaningful manner by understanding that different people have different needs and, as such, grow bonds with others in different ways. If these needs are considered and met on both ends, it facilitates the forming of trust between friends and romantic partners. What's more, it is also a matter of understanding what this factor is for you personally, and understanding that not everyone shares the same one. This is why Chapman suggests that we step outside of our own mindsets and what makes *us* happy, and consider which of the five "love languages" might apply to our friend or partner.

Lisa Fei takes Chapman's theories a step further. She believes that loving others (and yourself) with all five love languages is paramount. When you love someone with their primary and secondary love languages, but neglect the others, it's hard for your partner to feel truly fulfilled. If you're not receiving all five love languages from your partner, you'll likely be more inclined to fulfill your unmet needs by looking for it from someone else. This is not to say that some people don't have their preferences. Some might not respond at all to certain love languages. However, there is always some response to the love languages, even if it isn't their primary or secondary. Maybe some people don't love presents, but they receive the message and the meaning nonetheless, and they appreciate it if the gift is thoughtful and meaningful. Perhaps someone else isn't inspired per sey by consistent affirmation, but they might need to be reassured that they matter and that they're important every so often regardless. The important thing is that you step outside of yourself and show empathy to determine what these are, while being considerate and compassionate. At the end of the day, making the effort in terms of trying to truly understand someone, as well as delivery, timing, and sentimentality of the effort are what's really important.

For those who are unfamiliar with Chapman's Five Love Languages, let's take a moment to assess what they are and exactly what they entail in terms of building a thriving relationship:

Words of affirmation - offering verbal support and encouragement. If your friend or partner is feeling down and words of affirmation are their love language, make a point to remind them that they are loved and appreciated, how much they mean to you, that they are unique and special, that they are strong and they can get through this, that they are with it, and other phrases of this nature. Even if your friend or partner isn't necessarily sad, if words of affirmation are their love language, then letting them know that they're important and that you believe in them can go a long way towards making them happy.

Quality time - one of the more self-explanatory love languages. If quality time is your friend or partner's love language, then just spending time with them is affirmation enough to show them that they're important to you. It shows that person they have value if you schedule and dedicate your time to being them and sharing experiences with them. This is about more than just being in the same room as your friend or partner, but also putting down the phone and giving them your undivided attention. Participate in active listening (making thoughtful statements and questions, good eye contact, etc.), make plans and memories, and develop a routine that centers around this person (date night for partners, movie night, bowling night, or whatever else you can think of).

Acts of service - essentially this is just helping your friend or partner out. This goes back into showing them that you think they're worth your time as well as your effort. Offer your assistance when they need help, ask if they need anything from the store on your way over, cooking for them after they had a long day at work, things of this nature. Also perhaps consider helping your friend or partner with the things they don't like doing, or what they can't but you can, like fixing the plumbing or changing the oil in their car.

Physical touch - this love language may sound sexual, but that isn't really what it's about. For friends, this could mean an arm around the shoulder, a hug, a smooch on the cheek or the head, or a reaffirming shoulder squeeze or slap on the back. With a romantic partner, the physical touch love language gets a bit more intimate: kissing, cuddling, holding hands, running your fingers through their hair, scratching their back, and so forth. Physical touch is a non-verbal expression of love that releases oxytocin into the brain, which is the feel-good hormone that will be revisited in-depth later in the text.

Receiving gifts - gift giving to build bonds with your friend or partner is not just about showing them that they're worth your money and the time it took to get the gift (though that might be part of it). Moreover, you don't have to buy them another gift every day, and it doesn't always have to be an expensive purchase - it can even be home-made. What's important is that it shows them that you're considerate of their likes and dislikes and that you're always thinking of them. That said, if your friend or partner's love language is receiving gifts, it is vital that you be consistent about giving them gifts on important dates and holidays!

THE PYRAMID OF TRUST

It should be noted that most people have more than one. It certainly wouldn't hurt to try each one. Then, if you were to, for example, try giving someone a thoughtful gift when receiving gifts isn't their thing, it certainly couldn't hurt. The true point is to understand the importance of stepping back and looking at the person you're trying to bond with through an out-of-body lens, so to speak. John and Julie Gottman of the Gottman Institute for Marriage and Relationship Research and Therapy testify that the most effective part of the love languages is that it builds empathy in relationships by encouraging selflessness and looking at what makes your partner happy rather than yourself (Broster 2021). The fact of the matter is that generally, when people fail to take this step away from their own perceptions, they think "if this makes me happy, it will make them happy," and they try to force what makes them happy down the other person's throat. This method shows a lack of compassion and effort to try and understand the other person. It makes them feel like they aren't worth your effort.

Despite being called the "love languages," the theory is far from inapplicable to non-romantic interpersonal relationships, that is to say, friendships and familial relationships. Calling it a "love language" might be a bit sharp in the case of friends, but then again perhaps not. Even with friendships, it's important to consider what it is that your friend likes and how to grow your platonic bond. Granted, it might send the wrong message if one were to go online and take a love languages test with a platonic friend, but if you take the time to listen close in your conversations, which is another vital component to friendships that we will discuss later, it's not all that difficult to pick their brain and figure out what they like without the test.

If gifts seem to be what makes them happy, say they can't stop talking about how much they love the gift their significant other or their family got them, try to run with it, get them a gift when they're feeling down and they'll be sure to perk right back up, and definitely don't miss their birthday or any big holidays! However, being a good friend goes well beyond just getting them a meaningful gift, even if it is one of their love languages, thus where the secondary love language comes in. Helping them with something, talking them up with verbal affirmation, or a simple hug will be sure to help a friend out of their period of lowness, all while growing your bond of closeness and mutual trust. Along with these acts of selfless consideration for one's friend, one must also be reliable, or be there for them when they need such acts, as well as be consistent about it, and of course, use strong listening skills.

To put the theory into practice, relationship coach and psychotherapist Stefani Goerlich notes, "I have found that 8 times out of 10, whatever the issues are that my client-couples bring to the table, they are rooted in a fundamental misalignment in how each partner gives and receives love." Conflict is often caused by the communicative disconnect from couples failing to understand the way in which the other person expresses and wants to receive love and affection (Duncan 2020).

As such, Goerlich finds Chapman's five love languages to be a useful framework for building those communication skills and figuring out what each partner needs to be happy in their relationship. She attests that, "when I use the love languages concept with my clients, I explain to them that we have love languages that we 'speak' and love languages that we 'hear,'" therefore determining how each person expresses and desires to receive affection is extremely helpful in resolving many of the issues brought to her attention. Goerlich adds that like learning a new language, someone learning to adopt their partner's love language is about putting in the time and effort to learn, and that "people are only incompatible when they are unwilling to learn and respond to their partners needs."

THE PYRAMID OF TRUST

Applying the Five Love Languages to Personal and Professional Relationships

It's true that Dr. Chapman's five love languages are more widely known to be utilized for romantic relationships and even non-romantic relationships like friends and family. However, co-author Lisa Fei takes Chapman's theories to another level, and poses the question, "what if we were to apply the love languages to professional relationships?" What would that even look like? First off, who are we using these love languages on? Namely this entails coworkers, partners, investors and customers. Next, how do we apply them?

Words of affirmation are an easy one. Giving encouraging words to partners and coworkers can provide a huge boost in confidence and motivation. Phrases like "you're doing a good job," and "I really appreciate all your hard work," can mean the world to anyone, and goes a long way in building interbusiness trust. As for investors, clients and consumers and those who are investing their time and money in your brand and product, words of affirmation can make them feel good about themselves, and subconsciously encourage them to trust in your brand. For one, make a point to remember your clients - their names, their preferences, and so forth, then use that information to bring about a friendly air of familiarity when they're around. The human mind is habitual, so remembering your clients and making it so they don't have to repeat themselves every time they have an interaction with your business gives them comfort, and moreover makes them feel like more than just walking ATM machines (Rivas 2020). Then after every interaction, be sure to follow up with a verbal display of your appreciation for their business.

Next on the list is quality time. For partners and coworkers, this might mean checking in on them, meeting one on one, holding workshops, and overall being committed to participating with them. When you do this, be sure to fully devote yourself to the task, which means putting your phone down, being in the moment, and immersing yourself in the conversation (Rivas 2020). As for investors and customers, the quality time love language might take shape in the form of conferences, events, podcasts, participating on company forums and so on. It's important to participate with those who are investing their money on you and your brand, to show your values and build your credibility with them.

Gift giving is another one that applies well to the professional sphere. For those who are already with your company, it can help to give gifts, from financial incentives to company products as a means of motivation and showing coworkers and partners that you appreciate them and their hard work. It also might take the form of sharing useful blog posts, or giving your team the tools they need to facilitate their jobs like software for example, or perhaps in the event of a coworker's birthday, a cake for the office and a $50 Target gift card (Rivas 2020). For investors and customers, this might imply, say, giving away free products or coupons.

Acts of service is another great way to apply the love languages to building trust in business relationships. Especially in a professional setting, what could make someone happier than helping whittle down their list of daily tasks and making their job easier? If you have a moment to spare, you could offer to help someone that you're trying to build trust with - take one of their tasks, help out with their current task, or offer to get something for them like coffee or food. Then when it comes to investors and customers, anything you can do to facilitate their process of giving you their money will certainly be greatly appreciated, and will make your brand far more desirable. This might include purchasing upgrades on software and hardware to speed up transaction time, or perhaps updating your company website regularly.

Acts of service may also include displays of empathy. Take the time to get to know your team members on a personal basis. Get in touch with their emotions by checking in and asking how they're feeling. Be understanding, helpful, and accommodating where possible. Cover for your coworker if they have to go home and take care of their sick child, send a care package to a coworker who's laid up in the hospital, and other actions of this nature. As for customers and investors, this kind of goes back to quality time. Get to know your investors and customer base by holding events, participating in blogs, and giving them the ability to share their thoughts about your brand one on one. It might not always be positive, but good critique is important for the growth of your company.

Last on our list is physical touch. This is where things get tricky since you can't get overly touchy in the business world, but it is also important, however, to understand different cultural norms. Physical touch in the business world could mean a firm handshake or if you're close enough, an assuring hand placed on someone's back or shoulder, or even a hug may help instill a level of comfort and trust. It's important to note that people can be more or less affectionate based upon societal norms. For instance, in the Middle East, it's common for people to kiss those of the same gender on the cheeks upon each greeting.

Overall, the most important part of Dr. Chapman's love languages in both the private and professional spheres is the expression of empathy for others. The love languages are about stepping outside of your own perceptions and trying to place yourself in someone else's shoes, and trying to understand what makes them happy. If you can manage to do this, you will not only be starting an exchange of empathy and understanding, but you will also be showing the other person that they're worth the effort that it takes to try and understand them. It isn't always a simple task - we're the main characters of our own stories after all, but that's what makes this effort so appreciated, and that's what inspires trust in the people that you want to forge bonds with.

7

THE FOURTH LEVEL - INTERPERSONAL TRUST, PART 1

THE BASICS OF INTERPERSONAL RELATIONSHIPS

The base level of our pyramid is interpersonal relationships, and as with any pyramid, it is so large relative to the other levels, in this case because it is the most common and significant level of trust there is. One can hardly consider their life well-lived if it was one devoid of interpersonal relationships. They serve as the basis of human bonding and are vital to personal growth and support.

However, the question yet remains: how do we build such relationships? How do we make enduring and lifelong relationships with people who are ultimately worth the time and effort? What's more, how do we show others that we are worth that same time and effort in turn? There's a lot of ground to cover in this regard, so we're going to start with the most basic kind of interpersonal relationships, which is essentially non-romantic; community, family, and friends.

THE PYRAMID OF TRUST

For one, you have to maintain a certain level of integrity. People want to work with and be around people with integrity. If you lack this, what are the chances people will want to be around you? If you're kind of hypocritical or you don't adhere to your own values or morals, people probably aren't going to want to be around you, let alone trust you. You need integrity in order to build strong relationships, both personal and professional; it shows people that you care enough about honoring your word and overall just being real, practicing what you preach, so to speak. Integrity is a matter of intent and action, often in correlation with what you say. For example, say you're dating someone, but you come to find out that person has the intention of persuading you into something you don't want to do, even despite the fact that they previously made a promise to the contrary. That intention would inevitably disrupt your relationship would it not? Is that someone you want to talk to or spend time with? Absolutely not. The intent of your actions and the relationship you're building matter.

Another example of this is perceived intent. Many people do seem to perceive intentions from others that are not the case and make assumptions based off of these perceptions. For example, a lot of people assume that when another acts a certain way toward them, like getting nervous, playing with their hair or other nervous ticks when they speak, and being really nice, they must be flirting, and thus they must like them romantically. Sure, if someone is indeed flirting, they might actually like the other person. On the other hand, making this assumption falsely can lead to all manner of complications.

It's important to consider factors beyond the surface rather than jumping to such a conclusion and being considered presumptuous, which is another contrary to having integrity. People can be misjudged for their perceived intent. How can being considered presumptuous be avoided? As Dr. Chapman explains, we must step back and consider other alternatives, or in this case, different ways of communicating that cannot be interpreted as flirtatious. Perhaps they're just being friendly, maybe they display a nervous tick because they're nervous around new people and are trying to step outside of their comfort zone to make new friends. Consider ulterior motives. "Hey, that bartender is definitely hitting on me," one might say, but maybe they're in fact trying to just be friendly, perhaps even slightly flirtatious, It's not because they want to jump into your bed right after their shift, or because they want to be best buds, but rather they might just want a decent tip since their hourly wages are less than that of other employees. So to answer the questions, "how does one show the kind of integrity that makes people want to enter an interpersonal relationship with them, be it friendly or romantic? What does this look like?" It's really a simple matter of being considerate and true to your values and morals. It's not judging people based on unfounded assumptions, and holding true to one's values and morals.

Next, we come to reliability. Reliability is vital for appraising yourself and others' capacity for having an interpersonal relationship. The first factor of being a reliable person is essentially competency and self-value. You aren't going to pay someone without proper credentials and mentionable experience in web design to make your company website. In your personal life, you may have a friend or a family member that gives reliably-poor advice. If you know this about them, you may choose to look elsewhere if you're ever in need of guidance.

As reliability is a matter of one's competency, this also means following through with promises. When you say you're going to hang out with someone, don't blow off your plans just because something better comes up. When you say you're going to be somewhere for someone at a certain time, don't be late.

The next part of being viewed as reliable is being attentive. Ignoring friends and family can be as detrimental to your interpersonal relationships as blatantly pushing everybody you care about away. As such you have to keep in touch and be communicative in order to maintain strong bonds of trust. However, being attentive carries a twofold meaning. Along with maintaining a constant line of communication, you also have to be compassionate and be considerate of the other person's needs. Take the time to ask the important questions next time you call a close friend or cherished family member - "how are you? What's going on in your life? How are you feeling lately?" If they aren't doing so great, then you may consider taking a page out of Chapman's book on the five love languages. Get them a present if gifts make them happy, or reassure them with affirming language if that's their style.

Next, look for opportunities to create memories with a person by establishing emotional connections to the things they like, for those are the moments that people remember. Instead of asking people out to coffee like everyone else, say, "Hey, where would you like to go for lunch?" "What cuisine do you like?" or "What food do you like?" (or at least that would work with me, because I love food). Find shared likes, hobbies, passions, or whatever else, and use these to create shared experiences. Creating memories is one of the best ways for two people to form a bond, because when this happens, the person associates the positive memory with the other person, thereby creating the same feeling for that person, and thus a bond of trust.

As previously mentioned, you must consider personal value, what yours is to the person you're trying to bond with and vice versa. What value are you creating for the other person, their emotions, their hopes, their needs, and perhaps even those around them. As shallow as it might seem to hear out loud, it's important to think about what you're getting out of the other person, and what they're getting out of you. As with professional relationships, it's a law of equivalent exchange.

Another great way to form connections is through active listening. A study was done that said if you give someone fifteen minutes of undivided attention, every single day—whether it's your wife or husband, your kids, or the key people in your life—it will drive everything when it comes to building trust and the relationship as a whole. In general, people simply *don't* listen, so suffice it to say that it takes some effort to do so. When you're in a phone conference or a meeting, and you're the one talking, you can't be assured that because you are saying something that everyone is giving you their undivided attention. When you think about that, it may be a bitter pill to swallow. It can kind of make you feel unwanted. Though, when you do listen to someone, you can make someone feel important and wanted, you may even change their world.

So how do you participate in active listening that gets results? For some, what it comes down to is curiosity. Listening to other peoples' stories and absorbing their knowledge and experiences is a great way to learn about someone and one of the best ways to go about forging a bond of trust with them. Being curious shows that you have genuine empathy for the person with whom you are speaking. People can really pick up on that curiosity and, most of the time, it makes them feel comfortable enough to share what's important to them. When they know you're listening, they are more likely to trust you.

What do think makes some people more likely to be promiscuous, or otherwise think that it's acceptable to cheat on their partner? One of the biggest reasons is related to the feeling of low self-esteem and feeling unwanted. This can be a result of mere neglect, though also from one person in a relationship not receiving affection in the way that they interpret as affection, referring again to Dr. Chapman's love languages. This can also be the result of a lack of balance in a relationship. If one person is in charge of everything in a relationship, from making the decisions to being the designated bread-winner, it can put strain on both people by making one or the other feel unappreciated (FrackingFreeIreland 2019). If the need for feeling wanted or appreciated goes unmet, people will tend to look for it elsewhere.

Let's look at a well-known historical figure as an instance of this: Catherine the Great, Empress of Russia from 1762 to 1796. Originally she was a princess of Prussia and the ruling family in Germany. She was married off to the reigning emperor of Russia, Peter the III, in order to strengthen the bond between the two countries and to undermine Austria. The resulting marriage was an atrocity to say the least: not only did Peter fail to please Cathrine as a husband, he publicly scorned, demeaned, and disgraced her on a regular basis, and in return she loathed him with every ounce of her being. She took numerous lovers to fulfill her needs, one of whom, the love of her life Grigory Potemkin, aided her when she overthrew her husband in a coup d'etat and took the throne of Russia for herself in 1762. Hell hath no fury like a spouse's scorn, nor a spouse's vengeance. Luckily, this isn't the 18th century, and the concept of being in a relationship has come a long way through an increased understanding of psychology and relationship therapy. We may not have empires and kingdoms to overthrow when our partner fails to fulfill our need of feeling loved and appreciated, but in a way, our hearts are a kingdom of their own, with a throne of trust within.

When you're seeking to establish a relationship with someone, be it personal or professional, you have to ask yourself, "what need are they lacking?" Think about it this way: what do you think compels a person to steal? The obvious answer is that they don't have money. But is it really for the money? No. Even people who have money will steal, right? So, if it's not for lack of money, what is it? I promise you that it's a feeling of being unwanted in some shape or form in life. Our emotion drives everything. So, if you can manage to listen to someone while being mindful and conscientious, you can build trust with that person.

The art of being conscientious comes to some more easily than others. Some people are just natural-born good listeners. Think about any famous talk show host, like Oprah: natural listener, naturally curious. But if you fall in the other category, where being curious is not natural, you should make the attempt to become more curious. There are so many benefits. Interviewing people, for example, is a great way to learn about someone, same with reading biographies and listening to podcasts. If you're fully engaged in the conversation, you'll lose track of the time, ask some questions and listen some more. Once you're enthralled, it just comes naturally. It becomes this great giving and receiving cycle, and it's very active for both parties, which makes it a great learning experience.

Another note to make is that in face-to-face situations, it's also important to give people constant eye contact. This is the best way to show the person with whom you're speaking that not only are you listening to them, but that you are fully engaged in the conversation. A lot of communication is nonverbal, as most experts know, and by giving the speaker eye contact, you are sending them a clear message. You show your interest in them. These things build trust because the speaker knows you are actually listening.

The key component of active listening is proving that you are actually listening. Believe it or not, people are well schooled in the importance of eye contact, but that doesn't necessarily mean that they are listening. A great way to prove that you are listening to someone is to take mental notes and repeat back to the speaker something they just said. Otherwise, if you are interviewing someone for example, using part of what they just said to formulate a question is a great way to show that you are actively engaged in the conversation. Also, summarizing key points of discussion is another way to assure that the speaker is being heard and understood.

Now that you know the best ways to show someone that you care, and from this build trust, forging meaningful relationships with friends and family should be a breeze. Take this chapter to heart and go make stronger relationships, because at the end of the day, humans truly are social animals - we need close-knit support groups to conquer the trials of life, and the only way of having one is through building trust. Suffice it to say that interpersonal relationships, that is, friends and family that one can lean on and rely on are vital for reassurance, personal growth, and overall a life well-lived. Though, arguably even more complex and intimate than this is romantic interpersonal relationships, finding that one who supports, builds you up, and inspires you to become your best self.

8

THE FOURTH LEVEL - INTERPERSONAL TRUST, PART 2

THE NEUROBIOLOGY OF ROMANTIC TRUST

Anyone who's ever asked for relationship advice has been given at least one of these little gems: "you need to trust each other, trust is everything in a relationship, without a strong foundation of trust you can't have a healthy relationship." Though these common theories are far from invalid, they're far too broad for such an intricate subject as trust, which spans between both biology and psychology.

Trust is deeper than confidence that your partner won't stray. Holistic therapist and Clarity relationship expert Maria Sosa defines trust as "honesty, fidelity, loyalty, safety, certainty, without doubt, the belief that a person or something is honest and reliable. The certainty that there is or there will be dependability and follow through. This can also apply to the self, not just others. Your word is your bond." If a bond of trust is formed between partners it is vital to understand how deep the meaning and importance of that trust goes. To this end, the following chapter discusses the tenets of trust from a neurological and biological perspective. What's more, we will look into its overall impact on people's romantic lives, and how we can build that trust. Then, if at any point said trust is lost for whatever reason, we will seek to answer the question: is it really lost forever?

First off, it is important to understand exactly what trust means in neurological terms, as well as how it applies to the human psyche. From this understanding of where trust comes from, perhaps we can have a hope of understanding how to build it in our relationships.

It makes sense that the level of trust in a relationship would equate with the amount of love shared. From a psychological standpoint, trust and love are more than just codependent; in fact, one may even believe that they are one in the same. It is commonplace that the bliss of a new relationship increases dopamine, the "feel-good" protein of the brain. Though it is associated with love and lust, it may not necessarily correlate with trust and dedication, or at least not directly. On the comedown of a dopamine surge, something called the "Coolidge effect" occurs in animals whose neurology is akin to our own.

Tests performed on groups of rats show that animals with high dopamine levels do indeed show a higher desire to breed, though with different partners, even to the point where they get bored of partners that they've already mated with. This is what is known as the Coolidge effect. Though ethical implications prevent testing the same theory from being applied on a human test group, it can still be surmounted that dopamine levels aren't always going to correlate with an increase in cheating behavior. In fact, thanks to the process of the prefrontal cortex, dopamine created by the mesolimbic pathway, or "reward pathway," can work in tandem with other chemicals and neurons in our brains to help grow love and trust.

As explained by "The Love Biologist" Dawn Masler, "this [reward] pathway also incorporates our more recently evolved prefrontal cortex, the thinking, planning, and reasoning part of our brain. This allows us a degree of restraint. By adding the prefrontal cortex to the pathway, you now are not completely swayed by your biological urges. You're not running purely on instinct. You have the ability to judge, weigh, and calculate the benefits versus the costs of each decision."

Any notion that dopamine is the sole motivator for trust and dedication in relationships must be re-evaluated. However, when that dopamine stems from oxytocin levels and works in tandem with related neurotransmitters, it is a different matter entirely.

When it comes to the feelings of trust and love in particular, the neuropeptide known as oxytocin also rises. The molecule was originally extracted to help birthing mothers' speed along labor and increase the production of breast-milk at the turn of the 18th century. More recently, it was dubbed "the love molecule," and as such has been widely sold as a cure for the lovelorn. As it turns out, pumping one's self full of hormones can backfire quite easily, while it might increase feelings of closeness and intimacy it does come with some consequences.

According to neuroscientist and Clarity expert Dr. Sarah McKay in her writings from *The Women's Brain Book: The Neuroscience of Health, Hormones and Happiness,* "women who breastfeed display a 'mama bear' effect whereby they show more aggression when threatened. Other studies have shown oxytocin increases envy, gloating and anger, which, to be fair, are all approach behaviours. Anger focuses your attention towards the target of your anger, as does envy. It's not all love and cuddles, even the love molecule has a dark, immoral side." The same is true of naturally occurring oxytocin, though obviously not on the scale of shooting it directly up your nose in a nasal spray. In healthy and naturally occuring doses however, oxytocin in tandem with the ocean of chemicals and hormones that make up the psyche are essential for building trust.

THE PYRAMID OF TRUST

Oxytocin is, as put by Masler, "the neurotransmitter of trust, so slowly, as you're getting to know and trust someone, your oxytocin levels increase," therefore giving us that sense of assurance in our relationships, and with it the associated feelings of connection, security, and closeness. As you experience these moments and spend time with someone, this feeling grows steadily, drowning our psyches in sweet, warm oxytocin and dopamine. However, in order to build trust and love into something more permanent, you need more than a few neuropeptides floating around the cerebrum. Rather we need to build neurotransmitter receptors, since, "like all signalling pathways connecting body and brain, oxytocin and vasopressin can only exert their effect by 'locking in' to their receptors. And like all receptors, oxytocin and vasopressin receptors are regulated by genes, hormones, epigenetic factors and life experiences. It's never quite as simple as we would like," according to Dr. McKay. As the growth of this hormone concentration along with one's relationship goes on, the brain will after some time reinforce the receptors, creating a perpetual flow of the neuropeptides that affects how we think about our romantic partners.

From a consistent production of these hormones of trust and love, we create that "foundation of trust" we've been talking about, in the form of an actual, physical foundation of sorts in the brain. The dating period is the time in which these foundations are built up. When they are built and the oxytocin levels reach their pinnacle, it manifests in the form of falling in love. Likewise, if there is no release of oxytocin, there's no actual liking - only want at best, and "if the 'liking' isn't there once the 'wanting' fades, people set off in search for the next rush," says Dr. McKay. She continues, "a second neural network is recruited as true 'liking' sets in. This network is associated with attachment, empathy and emotional regulation. It turns out the deeply committed couples who remain in love not only continue to 'want' their partner, they quite like them too."

Take Sarah Michelle Gellar and Freddie Prinze Jr. from the cast of I Know What You Did Last Summer. The couple met on the show in 1997 and have been going strong ever since, now approaching 21 years of happy marriage. They attribute the success of their marriage to the quality time they spend together. In an interview with People magazine, Sarah elaborated, saying to "take the 10 minutes — put the phone down, have a cup of coffee together. Walk the dog at the end of the night. Read a story with your kids" (Rimm 2018). The more time the better, but every spare moment counts when it comes to building trust.

This buildup of receptors over time that compel us to become enamored with a person might be a contributor to what is known as the "mere-exposure effect," or the familiarity principle. This is described as the phenomenon in which people have a tendency to find attachment and comfort from items or people that they find familiar. This has been tested in regards to everything from shapes and sounds to paintings and written characters. In terms of intimacy, this theory applies to people as well. If this theory holds true, it would imply that the starting "liking" can be constructed, even if it isn't initially pre-existent. Though perhaps, this is a discussion for later.

One experiment that analyzed the effect of oxytocin in our brains uses prairie voles, a rodent known for exhibiting pair bonding behavior and monogamy in the wild. Unlike more closely-related species, the vole brain contains processors for oxytocin, compelling the animals to remain monogamous throughout their lifespan. However, scientists have found that when these receptors are obstructed, the vole reverts to the same mating patterns as its fellow rodents. Likewise, when other rodents are genetically manipulated to develop these processors, they tend to behave more along the lines of the prairie voles' mating habits.

THE PYRAMID OF TRUST

From this, it can be concluded that oxytocin is a vital component of building love and trust in a romantic interpersonal relationship. Furthermore, it should be noted that "oxytocin, working in concert with a host of neurochemicals, has been implicated in an extraordinary number of social behaviours and physiological roles.".

These behaviors, according to Dr. McKay include:

> suppresses stress hormones cortisol and noradrenaline, and slows heart rate
>
> facilitates paternal care
>
> modulates distress in pups (and children) separated from their mother
>
> decreases anxiety and depression via oestrogen signalling
>
> important for foetal heart development, and in adults protects against heart disease
>
> accelerates adult neurogenesis (in rodents)

Even considering the effects and the importance of oxytocin in regards to the neuroscience of trust and love, this still seems like a vast oversimplification. Simply accounting for oxytocin levels and their correlating receptors ignores biological differences that are extremely influential in regards to how we process oxytocin, and so too how we fall in love.

For women, this flow of oxytocin and dopamine are all that are required for reaching the pinnacle of love, neurologically speaking. Women are biologically able to build these relationships internally with relative ease. Further, when a woman has an orgasm, their oxytocin levels skyrocket them straight to the peak, throwing many women to the mercy of love afterwards. Perhaps this phrasing is a bit pessimistic for the topic of love and trust, but with good reason. From these great heights of oxytocin and dopamine levels, it can be difficult to descend, blinded by great trust and affection to potential problems and red flags. This is not to say that men can't be blinded by love, but how they get to that point is starkly different, and arguably more difficult in many cases.

For men, this path to love on the oxytocin train is hindered by many obstacles. For one, there is testosterone to contend with. In another experiment involving prairie voles, a male was injected with testosterone, the result being that they were less attached to their mate and that they mated with others. The processors in the vole brain are not unlike our own, and as such we can come to conclusions about our own brains by studying theirs. In this case, it is that oxytocin for men is dulled by testosterone. Though it may seem that it would be the opposite in that testosterone is what drives men to mate, the case is quite to the contrary. As such, when a man is able to fully commit himself to his partner, his testosterone levels plummet.

On top of testosterone, men have an interesting compound in their brains that differs from women called vasopressin, a neurotransmitter that is equally important as oxytocin for falling in love.

According to the U.S. National Library of Medicine and the National Institutes of Health, vasopressin "is associated with physical and emotional mobilization and helps support vigilance and behaviors needed for guarding a partner or territory," or in other words, singular dedication to a partner. This neuropeptide increases when a man is sexually aroused. For a man to reach that pinnacle of love, the development of processors for this too are paramount. It is shown that when receptors for this neurotransmitter are established and strengthened, through marriage for example, testosterone levels drop (Vasopressin, 2018).

Unfortunately, there's a twist: a man's vasopressin levels drop dramatically when he orgasms, meaning that if a man or their partner is too quick to jump into bed, it could potentially spell the doom of the relationship before it can even start. Suffice it to say that rushing into this aspect may not do a romantic relationship service as far as men are concerned. So on top of the need for oxytocin and dopamine, men also need a steady stream of vasopressin and testosterone. Perhaps men and women really are different creatures, or at the very least in regards to love and trust building.

Based on the previously mentioned biological information, how can people build trust and love in their relationships, using the lens of neurology? For women, it's a simple matter of first gaining initial trust, which can be difficult with the current social climate, and rightly so. From there it's a matter of building that trust, getting to know each other, and thus, increase oxytocin levels until receptors are established. Then when a woman is comfortable enough to let their partner into their bed and they can achieve orgasm, these oxytocin levels skyrocket to new heights.

As for men, the biological difference is somewhat more complicated. As it turns out, maybe there is some legitimacy to the antiquated idea that men need to be strung along, sexually speaking, in the earlier stages of the relationship. A man who moves too fast in this aspect can very well find his potential romantic interest thwarted by his own biological mechanisms. Receptors for neurotransmitters don't grow overnight regardless of gender - so since men need those receptors for vasopressin to fall in love, giving them time to grow before sex is optimal for creating love interest.

So we have gathered that the bonds of trust and affection stem from deep within our psychology and biology. It is a complex system of passing neurotransmitters through their respective receptor proteins and checking out with different sectors of the brain until they are released throughout the body, inspiring love, affection, sexual attraction, trust, and emotional comfort.

According to Dawn Maslar, founder of Biggie Bioscience and adjunct biology professor, this pathway starts with the receptors and mores to the hypothalamus, and "if the other structures along the reward pathway don't veto the response, it finally gets to the hypothalamus. The hypothalamus is responsible for releasing oxytocin and vasopressin, the neurotransmitters needed to fall in love. All these structures work together to continue the chase or to cause it to come to a halt. When you meet someone you like, your judge says, 'I find this person attractive,' the amygdala sounds an alarm to say, 'Hey, pay attention,' and the hippocampus says, 'Let's remember this.'" From this point, the ventromedial prefrontal lobe, the decision-making complex, or "judge" as Maslar calls it, makes the final decision on whether these neurotransmitters are released into the body. If all goes well, the cycle goes back another lap - the amygdala is activated making you swell with shyness and nervousness, and then to the hypothalamus to release oxytocin, vasopressin, testosterone, and dopamine, depending on our biology, making us a nervous mess in front of our partner, potential or otherwise, and compelling us to want to rely on and commit to this person (Maslar 2017).

9
THE FOURTH LEVEL - INTERPERSONAL TRUST, PART 3

THE BEHAVIORAL APPLICATION OF ROMANTIC TRUST

From this understanding of the inner workings of trust and love from a psychological and biological standpoint, one might find that they are at the very least comprehensible. Although, matters of the heart are never quite so simple. From a scientific perspective, the feelings of love and trust that we feel when we're with "the one," can be broken down into a chain of interacting chemicals, proteins, and neurotransmitters. However, as romantic philosophers will tell you, life would be a dreary thing if love was simplified into another scientific method. In this regard, our society which has been raised on the idea that love is a thing of deep beauty and meaning would agree. One might dare say that there is far more to love and trust than a mere neuroscientific breakdown. In the words of English philosopher Bertrand Russel, "the good life is one inspired by love and guided by knowledge." In application to modern life, this quote might mean that it is imperative to personal happiness that we navigate life with a passion for love as well as an understanding of it. Perhaps with the knowledge of how trust and love work neurologically, we can understand how to make our love lives flourish with passion as well as trust, though this leaves us with the application of said knowledge.

To this end, perhaps it is most beneficial to examine how to implement this knowledge towards therapy and behavioral science, and from here, the actions of our day-to-day from the dating scene to mature, committed relationships.

From a macro perspective, trust can be evaluated as a fluctuating status that may or may not exist in any kind of dyadic relationship. Trust can be gained, lost, regained, strengthened, or weakened. It is a highly arduous process to attain the trust of another, and an even more difficult task to salvage trust after losing it. Yet it is vital to maintaining a healthy love interest. In the words of Stanford Research psychologist and Clarity expert Dr. Diane Strachowski, "a relationship without trust is like a car without gas, it won't go anywhere."

Trust is something that requires a vast amount of effort to cultivate in any relationship. Clarity psychologist and sex therapist Dr. Kate Balestrieri described trust as "a multi-dimensional construct," and a "biological imperative." From this perspective, trust is imperative to survival, as well as a fundamental human desire. In relation to sex and relationship-building, however, trust becomes even more elusive. Dr. Balestrieri continued by saying that trust in sexual relationships is built upon personal values, communication, and motivations. Developing trust as it relates to sex must be undertaken through processes of safe experimentation and open communication. While building trust in relationships is approached collaboratively by partners, it cannot be developed without personal introspection and exploration of your partner's personal preferences, likes, and dislikes.

THE PYRAMID OF TRUST

Dr. Balestrieri continues by saying that sexual intimacy with a partner is rooted in basic principles of trust, and can be better understood by asking various questions, including:

What do you know about this partner?

What do you want to know about this partner?

Is it important to you that you have an understanding of where they're coming from? If so, do you?

Do you know what both of your hopes, expectations, and fears are?

Is your partner someone that you want to be with for a long period of time? If so, does that change how you feel about being sexual with them, now versus later?

Are you comfortable asking these questions to a person?

Have you talked about your sexual health profiles? If you haven't, *why*?

Are you holding back or are you afraid that they might get offended?

Do you feel comfortable when talking about sex in general?

When asking yourself questions through the process of trust-building, you may feel the need to pause and process information. At any point, evaluate your personal beliefs and values uncovered through the process of trust-building. According to Dr. Balestrieri, if you can't trust yourself, you will have a difficult time trusting your partner. If sexual intimacy between partners is based on trust, which is in turn based on a combination of hope, faith, dependence, and assurance, be sure to keep personal safety in mind throughout the process of that trust-building.

Don't be afraid to ask your partner difficult questions and closely examine the origins of their personal fears and mental blocks related to intimacy and trust, as well as associated boundaries, which are different from person to person. When these boundaries are crossed, according to Sosa, this further hinders that person's ability to put trust into the other. In regards to these boundaries, Sosa recommends that "instead of focusing on "high/low", shift to "what works/doesn't work" and tuning into how you feel after setting or failing to set boundaries. If you feel resentful often, chances are your boundaries are not working for you because they are too loose, and if you often feel isolated, chances are your boundaries aren't working for you because they are too rigid." She continues by saying that "when you honor yourself, your needs, your time, there's a certain sense of discomfort/guilt at first, but eventually that turns into power and ultimately self-trust." First and foremost, this self-trust and from this, self-love are important prerequisites to building trust in a relationship.

Dr. Strachowski states that "self-love is more like self-care, but in a deeper way. It's more about self-respect. If I say I'm going to wake up every day at 7:00 in the morning and work out, but I never follow up on my own commitments to myself, I would gradually come to learn that my word doesn't matter. So I have to trust myself, and trust that what I say I'm actually going to do."

Building trust for one's self is just as important as building it for another person, especially when going into a relationship. If you can't trust yourself, who can you trust really? When you adhere to your plans of waking up early and exercising in the morning you gradually build trust for yourself. When you bring this self-trust into a relationship with another person, you enter the relationship with "respect and a higher level of self esteem," according to Dr. Strachowski. Is it impossible to manage being in a relationship otherwise? Absolutely. Though behavioral psychology shows that self-trust facilitates the building of trust between partners.

Once self-trust is attained, one must transition to the next stage by examining how that same trust is built between partners. One might start to build trust in a relationship using the same techniques utilized in building *individual* trust, by holding true to your word. When you say that you're going to do something, don't make excuses and follow through. If you say that you're going to wake up at 7 in the morning and work out with your partner, do it. Otherwise, your word will surmount to nothing as far as your partner is concerned. If your word that you'll follow through with basic promises means nothing, who's to say that it will mean anything when you say that you love them or that they can trust you to be faithful to them?

The next factor to examine is individual attachment style, and how it affects individual attitudes on trust. Attachment style correlates with attachment theory, an ethological and evolutionary theory in psychology that analyses relationships between people in regards to early childhood development, suggesting that we need a beneficial relationship with at least one primary caregiver in order to become healthy and functional adults. The theory suggests that individual attachment styles are formed during childhood through early relationships and bonds. Therefore, the parent–child relationship is a highly-important bond that can influence future relationships, especially as children reach adulthood. "Attachment" can be viewed as behavior exhibited when an individual feels threatened or upset. To establish trust in a new romantic relationship, it may be helpful to critically evaluate past relationships with family members or friends formed in the early stages of development.

In doing so, experts in attachment theory such as Dr. Diane Strachowski, have compiled the differing styles of attachment into four generalized categories.

The first attachment style, and the most ideal for building healthy relationships, is the "securely-attached" person. According to Dr. Strachowski, this is the style in which a person "learned that their parents were available, attentive, responsive, and that they could overall trust their parents—when they needed something emotionally, physically or otherwise, they knew that the parent would be there for them." Thanks to their trust in the unconditional love they learned from their parents, that attitude allows them to transition that trust into their romantic relations during adulthood with relative ease. Unfortunately, this kind of perspective on trust does not come easily to everyone. Many cannot consider themselves so lucky as to have had a perfect connection with both of their parents in childhood, and this is reflected in adult relationships.

The second attachment style is what Dr. Strachowski calls "the nervous type," or the ambivalent-insecure type. This person may have received some support and nurturing, and one or both of their parents were there for them to give emotional support and need fulfillment, though it was not perpetual. A nervous type may very well have recieved love as a child, but this attachment style stems from inconsistent or irregular care from parents. When this idea of trust transitions into their adult relationships, they may expect that their partner will be loving and emotionally supportive, though not all of the time. As a result, they may remain hypervigilant, as their nervous system and attention are wired to observe and focus on these patterns. Dr. Strachowski offers an example, saying "you said you were going to call but now it's three minutes

THE PYRAMID OF TRUST

later, and you haven't - and so I become already fearful of a response that you're not going to follow up, because that is what I learned from my childhood." So in short, our romantic relationships are going to tend to mimic that which we had with our parents. We are therefore more dependent on our romantic partner to replicate this than we would with, say, a close friend. As such, the expectations for our partner are going to be higher, along with the level of disappointment and distrust should they fail to meet expectations.

The next attachment style is the "avoidant" type. Dr. Strachowski likens this person's anxiety level to the prior style, though with a modicum of self reliance. This person will "auto regulate, they calm themselves down - they say, leave me alone, I'm good by myself. They also don't trust people implicitly, because their parents were more or less checked out." She also notes that this may have been a product of culture, saying "it could be an idea that children should not be coddled therefore teaching them that they should fulfill their needs on their own." Regardless, this style can be attributed to experiences of neglect, and as a result this type of person brings a policy of non-trust to their adult relationships, believing wholeheartedly in the idea of "if you want something done right, you have to do it yourself." This person struggles with being vulnerable and sharing because their emotional needs have been previously unfulfilled, they may have never learned how to do so independently.

The final attachment type that Dr. Strachowski notes is the least common, and is used to classify those who grew up in an environment of neglect and abuse: the disorganized-insecure attachment type. The parent or parents who were supposed to be protecting and nurturing their child instead hurt and abused them, and as such, their adult relationships are mired in distrust. Even with someone who is open and caring, the concept of trusting another person may be uncomfortable or unfamiliar. Instead, they seek the homeostasis of the dysfunction that they are familiar with, creating a habit of building toxic relationships with their partners during adulthood.

It can be expected that individuals classified by the final three styles of attachment might have some difficulty forming bonds of trust, and therefore, strong and healthy relationships. This conclusion reflects the significant impact of early life on the development of adult relationships. How we were raised is vital to the development and function of future relationships, highlighting the importance of understanding the psychology of who we chose to commit to. A relationship with two securely-attached people in a relationship is ideal, though as anyone who's been in a relationship knows, not everyone can be so lucky. However, it has been found that securely attached people are also compatible with pretty much any other style of attachment, perhaps save the style that mimics childhood abuse and trauma - and even then it would be more ideal than said person being with any other kind of attachment style. A securely attached person can emotionally support any other kind of style, raising them up and inspiring them to be better, more trusting, and self-reliant. Relationships between people that fall within the latter stylistic categories may not necessarily be doomed to fail, though if attachment theory is to be believed, they will certainly require some amount of effort in building trust and love.

With this point of attachment-style considered, it's important to note that it isn't impossible to work around complex attachment styles to cultivate thriving romantic relationships. It's certainly not uncommon to rise above negative habits learned from adolescence, and rather use them as an example of how *not* to approach relationships. Dr. Balesrieri recommends making a list of how our parents may have been dishonest during our youth and to "write down those behaviors, the words that they chose, the things that they would do, and the kinds of triggers that would lead them to lie." She continues, "did mom or dad only lie or get deceptive if they were trying to put food on the table for their kids, or was it more around retaliation and getting even with people? Explore what these behaviors were and what the motivation was for them to the best of your knowledge, and create a blueprint for behaviors that are not compatible for you and a partner." If you start exhibiting these kinds of behaviors that you deem negative for your relationship, perhaps it's time to do some self-reflection and engage in dialogue with your partner about how to make positive changes. Should your partner start exhibiting familiar negative behaviors, it might be time to talk about working on some changes as well, or otherwise take some time to logically consider concluding your relationship, assuming nothing can be done.

So, how can you tell if your partner is trustworthy? You can certainly make the initial judgement based on your general gut-instinct, or consider their upbringing and how it might affect how they will operate in a relationship. You could even look at how they have navigated their past relationships.

It is important to remember that a partner's upbringing does not always directly correlate with trustworthiness or general relationship satisfaction. Maybe they didn't have the best relationship with their parents, but it's possible that they turned this negative into an example of what not to do, rather than carry it with them into adulthood. Even if they initially displayed poor tendencies in their past adult relationships, they may have grown and evolved. What matters is the present.

As Dr. Strachowski puts it, "Do their actions match? Do their words match their actions or behaviors? So if I say we're going to go to the movies and I don't follow up, you're going to wonder what happened there, right?" The question that one should truly ponder in such a situation is, "is this person truly trustworthy," and, "if this person is going to let me down on something as trifling as, say, going to the movies, what's to say that they won't betray my trust in regards to something more significant, like being unfaithful?" If you catch a partner betraying your trust and they give you a canned response or tired excuse are they actually going to take responsibility for their mistake and follow up, or will they simply return to old habits once the conflict passes? If they have some level of insight into their behavior and can communicate with you about their emotions, thoughts, and needs, both emotionally and sexually, you're likely going to trust them more.

When it comes to trust-building, consistency is vital. Returning to the matter of parental example and upbringing, if a partner's consistent behavior aligns with consistent parental support, perhaps this person may indeed be worthy of trust. What's more, if their behaviour is consistently positive and worthy of trust, does it not stand to reason that they deserve your trust? Then obviously when that behavior shifts, perhaps it's time to examine the relationship. To what degree did your partner's consistency shift? Has the new behavior become consistent, and is it negative or positive? Both consistency and trust are components of an intimate relationship that can have a tendency to shift, which is why mindfulness and communication about them are so important.

What about their *vibe*? Though often associated with modern vernacular, the word "vibe," originally an abbreviation for "vibration," has been used to describe instinctive feelings individuals experience. In other words, what does your gut tell you about a person? Dr. Strachowski suggests that, "you should consider your head, your heart, and your gut when making decisions…if you're going to make a long-term commitment to someone, your gut is more what we consider your

THE PYRAMID OF TRUST

intuition. That's your feeling about someone. And some people have a good gut."

Then again, not everyone has a good gut. The key is to turn inward and analyze what kind of person you are and if your gut is worth trusting. If you're a secure, functioning person, and you have a good feeling about someone, go ahead and trust your gut and intuition. If you're the nervous person and your gut is all over the place from bring nervous and wired all the time, then it would be worth a second look. If you're making decisions about someone and you're up and down all the time, then perhaps you may need to calm down first. In this case, you need to hone your intuition and make sure that you're using more than just your gut, but also your power of rationality.

Ask yourself, "Are we a good team? What do we have in common? Do we share the same values? Do we want the same lifestyle? In your heart, do you have positive feelings towards this person?" If the answers to these questions reveal red flags, perhaps it's time to consider moving on. You have to give these decisions time and careful consideration. This goes for the complicated decision to end a relationship, as well as the decision to fully invest in a partner.

Another important subject, and one to consider when making a decision on whether a partner or potential partner is worthy of emotional investment, is the concept of "betrayal trauma." Betrayal is truly an insidious thing that is emotionally draining, to the point that it can reduce a person to a mere shell of who they once were. More importantly, it is something that you need to remain cognizant of when your partner is going through it, presently or in the past, because its impact on the overall relationship is undeniable, and as such has to be addressed at one point or another.

Dr. Balestrieri describes it as "a series of behaviors that happened outside of the relationship and not directly to your person more often than not, and so it can feel really offending, because unlike a physical or emotional abuse or financial coercion, betrayal is not always something that happens person to person. It happens behind your back to one extent or another." One might catch their partner in the act of betrayal, though may provoke questions of the previous, undiscovered betrayal. It's like catching an employee stealing from the register. The question is not why they stole, but how long they have been doing so. Balestrieri continues by detailing the fact that "there are a lot of implications for betrayal trauma, including how someone views themselves, how they view the world and how they view relationships. It can create a sense of unreality, because everything they thought was true in their relationship is not, and that can feel really jarring and confusing and discombobulating. People who suffer betrayal trauma often will struggle with their own identity and how they construct who they are and how they want to be in relationships."

There are even physical ramifications of betrayal, whether you are the one betrayed or the betrayer, such as loss or increase of appetite and sleep, nausea, increased sweat response and heart-rate, and even sexual dysfunction. There are emotional effects as well, including feelings of "shame, anger, rejection, that you're not good enough, scared, worried, and sad." All of these compounding emotions overwhelm the senses, forming an intense, emotionally-deteriorating experience. There are few things in this world more damaging to one's trust and damning to future relationships than having your heart broken while in an emotionally-vulnerable state. In some cases, this can lead to strong feelings of self-doubt or suicidal ideation. It can make you question the point of seeking out another romantic relationship. Even if you're brave enough to become available after a particularly painful experience, it can be difficult to let a new partner get close for some time due to lingering feelings of distrust and insecurity. Sometimes this betrayal trauma can be so emotionally destabilizing, it can

THE PYRAMID OF TRUST

even lead to the person who was once cheated on becoming a cheater themselves in later relationships.

Make no mistake. When you put trust in someone, you're essentially leaving your emotions in their hands with the hope that they're competent and trustworthy enough to do well by your decision. Regardless of whether you put trust in someone in a personal or a professional setting, when that person betrays that trust, it's a traumatic experience on a psychological and even physical level. If someone betrays you and you don't experience such an impact, you might wonder if you're just putting on a strong face, or whether you really even trusted that person in the first place. This chapter skims the surface of how betrayal and betrayal trauma is something you should take into consideration when you're trying to figure out if a person is worth giving your trust to on an interpersonal level, though this leaves more to be desired. We are left with the questions: what happens when trust is lost? Can it be restored? In the next chapter, we will take a look into answering these questions, in regards to both professional as well as interpersonal relationships.

10

THE LOSS AND RESTORATION OF TRUST

LOSS AND REBUILDING OF PROFESSIONAL TRUST

When a professional type of trust is lost, it can cause great harm to you and your brand name. Loss of this trust can burn bridges between your brand and potential consumers and even potential investors or partners, be it in the name of self-interest or otherwise. However, unlike the previous two levels, it is not near impossible to rebuild.

The Wells Fargo cross-selling scandal is a great example of this. For those who don't know, there were circulating rumors starting in 2013 of Wells Fargo employees in California that were caught creating millions of new checking accounts and hundreds of thousands of credit card accounts under existing customers' names without their consent or knowledge in order to meet their strict quotas. After thorough investigation, the scandal truly came to light in 2016, during which time the bank was forced to pay $185 million to the city of Los Angeles, the Consumer Financial Protection Bureau, and the Office of the Comptroller of the Currency. What's more, 5,300 of the low level employees who created the fake accounts were fired, along with CEO John Stumpf, who also had to pay $41 million dollars in reparations on top of that. Wells Fargo lost 2 percent of their stock value, as well as a vast amount of public trust because of the scandal. Through this, as well as being caught in a number of other scandals that took place afterwards, Wells Fargo has continued to persevere. After reparations were made, they even attempted to regain public trust by putting out several commercials guaranteeing their integrity and the security of their customer's accounts. If this isn't a perfect example of a business losing credibility and trust, surviving, and bouncing back, one can scarcely imagine what is.

Loss and Rebuilding of Interpersonal Trust

One might ask, "How could anyone think that deceit and betrayal is acceptable, and where does it come from psychologically?" It is generally a skewed and indirect expression of needs and wants. From what has been reviewed to this point, we can surmise that a tendency to be deceitful is based on experiences during the early stages of development. At some point, one may come to the conclusion that they can't get what they need by being honest and asking directly. Instead, they may have found that acting *indirectly* is a more productive method.

Using this strategy, "they derive a sense of power, or they're able to eradicate some shame, or they're able to kind of exercise a sense of getting away with something and feeling more in control and like they have a little secret, something that's theirs to hold on to, or they really just get to have a need met in a way that is, in their minds, the safer strategy, rather than being direct and risking rejection or being shamed, critiqued, or let down," to quote Dr. Balestrieri.

As a result, they have come to be unable to communicate what they need and what is upsetting to them, to say "I feel very frustrated right now, and here's what would help me find solutions." Overall, it is an impulse, a psychological reaction to scarcity, shame, neglect, resentment, insecurity, or disempowerment.

Regardless of what type of betrayal may have been experienced, it's a difficult matter to move forward from, especially if the relationship in which the betrayal occurred is continued. That said, it is far from impossible to repair damaged trust. First and foremost, what is required for making these repairs, according to Sosa, is motivation and dedication. She says that "there needs to be a commitment to working on the relationship. The partner who has betrayed the trust has to be willing to be able to do what must be done to repair, and the partner who has been betrayed has to be open to accepting the attempts." The next most important tool according to Sosa, is patience.

A lack of patience can manifest into a serious impediment to healing and regaining trust in the relationship. According to Dr. Balestrieri, "the person who has betrayed the other needs for things to be okay, faster than a betrayed partner is often ready for things to be okay." This can become a consequential issue because every person needs to heal at their own pace, and if attempts are made at expediting this process, it can result in more problems, further trauma, and in many cases, the end of the relationship.

One example of what not to do in such a predicament, as advised by Dr. Balestrieri, is the piecemealing of information from the betrayer to the betrayed. The person who did the betraying may believe that they're saving their partner from being overwhelmed by information regarding the betrayal event, but in actuality, they are not only prolonging the process of healing, but making matters worse by preventing their partner from fully understanding what took place. This inevitably results in new trauma, and even further distrust. Then, things can be further soured by the aforementioned desire of the betraying party for their partner to be okay, and the restoration of equilibrium. This unfortunately can manifest in the form of belittling the other person's feelings, or manipulating the logic of the situation to make that person question their own sanity - otherwise known as "gaslighting." If that person brings the betrayal up a year later, the person who betrayed them might say "why can't just you let that go? It happened forever ago, get over it." Again, this is dismissive of the person's feelings and sanity, which can make the damage from the past resurface or even create new traumas.

The solution to previously-established quandaries, according to Dr. Balestrieri, requires empathy and patience between partners, and involves taking the time to communicate and heal as a couple. The arduous healing process can feel an eternity of dysregulated emotions from both partners, and the slightest misstep can open disastrous new wounds or prolong the healing process.

Relationships are rarely perfect, but if both partners believe that their love is worth fighting for, these obstacles can be overcome with patience, understanding, hard work, and communication. With any hope, the relationship will be fortified through the process of trust-building.. It may never again be the same, though that's not necessarily a bad thing. Instead, couples will find themselves in a relationship reborn, with new transparency and strengthened bonds. Dr. Balestieri likens this renewal to an art form in Japan where, if a vase is broken, it will be resealed with gold rather than discarded. The vase will never look as it once did, but it can still be functioning and beautiful in a new way and perhaps may be even stronger than before.

Rebuilding trust on as grand a scale as utter betrayal can't simply be done with equally-grand gestures. Rather, it's all about the day-to-day actions and staying in sync with one's partner through the arduous process of coming to trust each other again. Dr. Balestieri suggests two major ways of reforging that trust:

1. DON'T MAKE PROMISES YOU CAN'T KEEP.

In hopes of a quick fix to relationship problems, and fear of disappointing a partner, people can sometimes have a tendency to overpromise. However, this has a way of backfiring, as promises often have a funny way of coming up short - fact is, sometimes things happen that are out of your control, and when these things come up you can't always hold to your promises to the letter, if at all. During this time of cooperation and healing, it is detrimental to be breaking your promises, piling further lies onto the list of reasons why your partner may feel distrustful. Therefore, it is vital to be conscious of what promises you can and can't keep, and when you can't, you must be honest. It may be disappointing to your partner when you say you can't uphold your promises perfectly, but not nearly as much as saying you can and failing to uphold that. It is important to be realistic. If they ask you to meet them at a certain time and it's looking like you'll probably be late, set a new plan to meet when you know you'll be available. If they can't trust you to keep simple commitments, how can they expect you to keep larger ones such as, say, not betraying them again?

2. BE HONEST AND COMMUNICATIVE ABOUT FEELINGS AND NEEDS

When feeling scared, angry, frustrated, or resentful, or repressing emotional or sexual needs, it's impossible to keep feelings concealed for long periods of time. Over time, repressed feelings can surface and cause tension in a relationship as transition to frustration and resentment. Therefore, it is important to talk about personal problems or unfulfilled needs in a manner that is not accusational, defensive, or reactive. In doing so, couples can process shared issues out with calm, reason, and consideration, eventually moving forward in a productive way. This is highly imperative because betrayal generally occurs as a result of a "mostly unconscious expression of resentment or anger about something," says Dr. Baletieri. To ensure that it never happens again, this subconscious expression of frustration and resentment needs to be extinguished at its source. Dr. Baletieri continues, "when you can align yourselves like that, implicitly, your nervous system feels like it's got a partner in crime, and somebody's got your back." At the end of the day, love is about having a companion with whom one can confide, someone to navigate the tribulations of life as and revel in the successes.

3. Consider Your Partner's Love Languages

The final point applies to building the initial trust in a relationship as well as rebuilding it if trust was broken. You have to consider Dr. Chapman's Love Languages. It is certainly important to learn that what makes you happy isn't necessarily what's going to make your partner happy, and from this, one can at least make the attempt to understand their needs. If your partner likes gifts, make a point to be consistent about buying them presents. If words of affirmation are what makes them feel loved, make the time to sit them down and tell them how much they mean to you and how amazing you think they are, and so on. What's more, it takes a lot of effort to step outside of one's own personal notions and perceptions to consider the wants and needs of another person. The exertion of that effort shows your partner that you're trying, and regardless of what stage of the relationship you're in, that display of effort can mean the world to them. From this, one will notice a further increase of trust.

11

THE FOURTH LEVEL - INTERPERSONAL TRUST, PART 4

CONCLUSIVE THOUGHTS

Feelings of trust and love in romantic interpersonal relationships are created by specific neurotransmitters in the brain, and what transmitters are required for the building of these feelings are determined by gender-based biology. What's more, these neurotransmitters require receptors that they can lock into in order to impact the psyche and fully establish themselves as feelings of trust and love. For women to build said feelings, their neurology requires the neurotransmitter oxytocin, which compels trust and dedication, and from this the dopamine that is released from seeing, touching, and being with the person for whom their oxytocin flows. Therefore, when women spend long periods of time with their partner, trust and love increase with the strengthening of receptors for oxytocin and dopamine. Their oxytocin levels spike when they experience an orgasm. Men on the other hand, require not only oxytocin and the correlated dopamine release, but also vasopressin, a neurotransmitter that compels dedication to a singular partner. Furthermore, it is important to note two more factors that differ by gender. First, male testosterone blocks the effects of oxytocin, which is why young men with high testosterone levels might prefer sleeping around to settling for one partner. Next, is that higher vasopressin levels leads to a fall in testosterone levels, which explains certain changes in men after committing themselves, such as a tendency for weight gain after getting married. When these receptors are severed for one reason for another, testosterone levels rise once more, explaining why men who are freshly divorced become so eager to get back to the dating scene. On the down side, men's vasopressin levels drop dramatically when they orgasm, and so too their desire for building bonds of trust and love, which is why it's so necessary for building bonds of love and trust that men's vasopressin receptors are established before succumbing to the throes of passion.

When applied to the behavioral psychology of relationships, building initial bonds of trust and love are a matter of applying time and effort. Couples spending time together is the most straightforward way to build those receptors for the neurotransmitters associated with trust and love, though the day-to-day issues that might arise make things a bit more complicated than that. For love and sex, it is imperative to do the following four things:

Communicate needs and desires, as well as fears and frustrations regarding sex and the overall relationship, in a calm, open, and reasonable manner.

Be considerate and understanding of your partner's wants and needs, emotionally and sexually. Learn who they are and what makes them tick - what they want and need obviously, as well as what makes them happy or sad, and what their boundaries are; that is, what they're willing to do as far as your needs and wants are concerned and what they might be uncomfortable with.

Be open to meeting with your partner halfway on what both of your needs and wants are, or perhaps even changing yours all together in certain regards to accommodate them.

Give your partner reason to trust you through the small, daily things, such as being present when you say you're going to be. If they can't trust you in regards to smaller needs, how can they rely on you for more important matters, like not cheating?

It is also important for building trust in a relationship that you have to trust in yourself. When you make commitments for, say, changing habits for the purpose of self-improvement, you have to be able to trust yourself to follow through. If you can't trust yourself, you certainly couldn't expect someone else to trust you. Likewise, how can you trust someone else if you can't trust yourself?

The next point worthy of consideration is how to determine if someone is worthy of trust, whether one is considering investing initial trust, or otherwise deciding if their already established partner is worth continuing to place their trust in. Obviously one can simply rely on their gut-feeling towards the person, though this requires some self-introspection. It's important to question the dependability of your gut feelings first and foremost. Next, take the necessary time to think things through, and pair that gut-feeling with reason and logic. Ask yourself how compatible you are with this person, if you have similar desires, goals, and values. Ask if you are comfortable with this person and if the positive feelings and interactions outweigh the negative. Then, consider the person's track record with previous relationships, and as such, their tendencies in regards to commitment. What is their attachment style? That is to say, what was their relationship like with their caregivers, how has that transitioned into their later adult relationships, and more importantly, how has that transitioned into your relationship? If all or most of the answers to this line of questioning are positive, then maybe this person is worth putting some trust in and seeing where it goes.

When it comes to the matter of rebuilding trust once the initial trust has been tainted or lost due to betrayal, assumedly by being unfaithful in one aspect or another, matters can become even further perplexing. If you are the person who was betrayed, consider potential contributing factors that may have caused them to do so before throwing in the towel on the relationship. Again, what was their relationship like with their parents, and how has this transitioned into how they navigate adult relationships? What are possible underlying issues that might have been repressed in the current relationship, culminating in the final act of betrayal? What steps can be taken to ensure that it never happens again? Whether you were betrayed or the betrayer, communication is particularly vital to reforging lost trust. There must be an effort to maintain an open line of communication from both parties in regards to what is causing fear and frustration in the relationship. What's more, there needs to be honesty when it comes to promises and whether or not they can be kept, especially for the person who initially caused the distrust in the relationship. If a promise cannot be kept, be it as simple as being somewhere when you say you will, or complicated as making necessary shifts in behavior, honesty in the matter is vital to the survival of the relationship. Patience also is just as important as honesty and communication. Everyone heals at their own rate, and trying to rush that process along can manifest in the form of belittling or gaslighting, which can cause further damage to the relationship, and the potential resurfacing of the initial trauma. However, with patience, honesty, and communication, wounds can be healed and trust rebuilt. The relationship may not be the same afterwards, but it will be made anew as one that is just as strong, if not more so.

Overall, the importance of trust in regards to building a healthy and meaningful relationship is on par with love itself. In fact, they're two sides of the same coin. One simply cannot exist without the other. From a psychological and neuroscientific perspective it's a series of neurotransmitters that are produced when you find that special someone, and over time, those neurotransmitters develop receptors to latch on to, resulting in feelings of trust and love. Humans aren't voles, so trust is not something that we're hard-wired to feel, which is why it's important to keep this neurological perspective in mind. It emphasises the fact that building trust doesn't come effortlessly, which is why patience, consistency, and dedication are so important when building that trust in our relationships. When this knowledge transitions to the application phase, things become a bit more complex, but the need for patience, consistency, and dedication remain the same. Whether gaining initial trust, or rebuilding that which was lost, this overall effort needs to be applied to every aspect of the relationship - from forming strong foundations built with honesty, to slowly building bonds of trust over time through understanding and open communication in regards to each partner's needs, emotionally as well as sexually. With aforementioned patience, consistency, and dedication to the relationship, there is no reason why the rest should not come easily, propelling us towards stronger bonds and healthier and more meaningful relationships.

12

INTERLUDE

What have we learned about the seemingly all-encompassing subject of Trust (with a capital T)? We know that trust is heuristic, meaning that it allows us to make quick decisions rather than be held up examining every possible contingency, or "paralysis by analysis."

When examining the fragile needle of trust, this mental shortcut allows us to automatically place dependence on another and count on them to be honest and fulfill our needs (whatever they may be), rather than allowing our mind to be drowned in the what ifs, like "what if my partner is cheating on me," or "what if my new business partner ends up screwing me over." It can be so easy to become mired in doubt, which is what makes trust so essential for moving our lives forward. Of course, trust can be broken, far more easily than building it, but you can't use that possibility as an excuse to constantly withhold trust.

It is essential that the four components of trust be considered when building these essential bonds with others. Without these, regardless of what kind of trust you're trying to build, it will inevitably fail. Building trust is a matter of effort exertion, and these four components are essentially how that effort resonates. You have to be consistent about exerting that effort. In your exertion of effort you have to show compassion

THE PYRAMID OF TRUST

and empathy for the needs of the person that you're trying to form a bond with. You need to be communicative about their needs and values in correlation with your own. Lastly, you need to show the other person that you're capable of fulfilling these needs.

The next point we covered was the harmfulness about the idea of independence and the need for dependence. The fact of the matter is that we're too social and our society too intertwined for us to not rely on others for support, in the personal as well as the professional sense.

Our pyramid of trust is composed of four levels: blind trust, authority trust, professional trust, and interpersonal trust. However, none of these levels can be achieved without the most basic foundational components of building trust: self-trust and credibility. Self trust is crucial to any other kind of trust, because if you can't trust yourself, you can't efficiently lend trust to others, nor can you expect others to trust you. This is built the same way one would build any other kind of trust. You have to be compassionate to yourself, as opposed to wallowing in self hate and pity. What's more you need to be honest with yourself, you have to show yourself that you're competent in following through with plans you set for yourself, and be consistent about making the effort. The next step of building a proper foundation is creating credibility for yourself. In regards to the public view, you can't do anything without building credibility, from getting a loan to growing a business. Likewise, you also need a sense of credibility when building relationships. If you're known as someone who's quick to betray, hypocritical, or just taxing to be around, no one will want to be in a relationship with you.

Then we continue to our pyramid of trust's structure itself. At the top we have blind trust, a complete suspension of reason in exchange for total faith. It can be used for good, like conducting an orchestra to perform at their best, a military commander who requires blind trust in their orders to manage a successful campaign, and so forth. If there is any doubt in the commands issued by such people, the whole of the operation falls apart. Then there's the way that blind trust is used for evil, including when people use blind trust to exploit and manipulate their followers. Though when those who command even blind trust lose their credibility, in situations such as public scandal or controversy, this trust is often the most difficult to rebuild. Blind trust intersects with the other levels, and when it does it can either drive large operations toward success, or if in the wrong hands, create a toxicity that in the end is unbeneficial for every party involved. Overall, it is ill-advised to apply blind trust to the other levels, particularly in regards to professional and interpersonal trust.

In regards to authority trust, or trusting in experts, celebrities and so forth, their position as such is entirely dependent on their credibility in the minds of the public that follows them, their public trust so to speak. If the consistency of their credibility waivers, their position as an authority is undermined. There are several ways in which one can become a figure of authority or expand their already existent position, mostly in the form of spreading one's name throughout the public in as many different forms as possible, communicating ones value and competency to those they are trying to appeal to, and their values in correlation with the values of their intended public.

Next comes the professional level of the pyramid. As a part of this level, you must build your credibility and that of your brand in a similar way that you would do so as a figure of authority. In a manner of speaking, you and your brand *are* an authority on whatever it is you're trying to pawn off to your chosen public, and to show them such, you need credibility. Loss of credibility can certainly hurt you and your brand, it can burn bridges to particular consumer bases, as well as potential investors and partners. That said, it is not impossible to regain this trust, though it is certainly still difficult. One can of course stick to the consumer base that sticks with them and try to expand in that market, otherwise reparations can attempt to be made through following the four components of trust and shifting brand values.

Last, though certainly not least, comes interpersonal relationships. First and foremost, you must take Dr. Chapman's Five Love Languages into consideration, a theory that dictates the importance of being considerate of your partner's or friend's personal needs when trying to build trust. Of course, it's important to know what makes them feel loved, though the theory is multi-beneficial. It shows the person with whom you're trying to build trust that you're trying to make the effort to step outside of yourself and your perceptions to understand how their own may be different. This is absolutely essential when trying to build trust because it shows that you think they are worthy of the significant amount of effort that goes into such a feat.

When it comes to basic interpersonal relationships, like with friends and family, there are several ways to build trust, including integrity and reliability. Integrity is a matter of what you say aligns with what you do, and how this correlation between the two is perceived by others. Don't be a hypocrite when you have established values that would imply otherwise. Don't betray the other person while saying that they mean something to you. When you say you present some value to the other person, follow through with it. Say what you mean and mean what you do. Reliability on the other hand, relates back to the four components of trust. You have to make time for people that you want to build trust with, be there for them when they need you, be compassionate towards them, and be consistent in all of these actions.

When it comes to romantic interpersonal relationships, the complexities expand even further. One needs to have a basic understanding of the psychological implications of building trust between romantic partners, and why the need for it has been hardwired into our psyches since the dawn of the human race. I dare not repeat the long spiel required just to scratch the surface on the neuroscientific complexities that go into having a firm grasp of building love and trust in the human psyche. That said, it is integral to building romantic trust that one has an understanding of just how trust is built psychologically, and how it differentiates along the lines of genetics.

Next, you have to consider how this information is put into play, as well as how to gauge the trustworthiness of your partner or potential partner. Then, as is quite common, the initial trust is bound to be broken in one form or another, and like the other levels of trust, it is not an easy task to mend it. However, interpersonal trust is hands-down the least irreparable of the previous three. With a shift in mentality (in correlation with Dr. Chapman's Love Languages), some solid emotional exertion through communicating what needs to be changed, making the effort to consistently adhere to the needs of your partner and a little compassion, there is no reason a bond once shattered cannot be reforged. It will not be in the likeness that it once was, but it will be born anew, a shared experience that is stronger and more mature than before.

Trust is the very thread that holds us together in all of the most important aspects of our lives. It is imperative to know how to build it up in our professional and personal relationships, and harness that ability in order to create a high quality of life through accomplishing goals and fulfilling emotional needs. Trust is something that seeps into

every important aspect of life since the beginning of time. It allows us to not have to over-rationalize every little thing in our lives, and on a grander scale, it moves us ever-forward into the horizon of the human race. Bonds of trust unite people in common interest and values, from leaders and authorities with their public, to business leaders with their consumers and investors, to friends with friends, and lovers with lovers.

Without trust, there would be no foundation for love or friendship, there wouldn't be professionalism or businesses working in tandem for shared interests, and there would be no confidence in the direction of teachers or leaders. Could it be that trust may be the very thing with the potential to unite all of human-kind? Perhaps mistrust is what stands between humanity and a global unity that we hear about in utopian literature. This is not to say that you should lend trust to anyone you meet haphazardly, though, to quote Ronald Reagan, "trust, but verify."

You now have the tools to ascertain your own conclusions on navigating, sustaining, and rebuilding that trust therein. Use it to forge your relationships to be the best they can be, and be in the driver seat of your success, happiness, and future.

ABOUT THE AUTHORS

Trust bestows us with the light of certainty. Without it, we would be left to stumble blindly through the darkness of the unknown in which life itself is mired.

Everyone knows that you can't have a relationship without trust, yet it is far more intertwined with our lives than can be sufficiently explained in a single cliche. Trust is more than an advantage or privilege, it is the foundation on which everything that matters in life is built. Attaining prosperity in life's relationships without trust is like flying a kite in the absence of wind—without it, we would never soar to our greatest heights. We must have a basis of trust for whomever we are dealing with, from a friend to a teacher, doctor, lover, and all the way to a business acquaintance and clientele. We depend on it to achieve fulfillment in any of these spheres.

Pyramid of Trust shows the importance of having the faith of others in your daily life. What's more, it aims to inspire you to lend that trust to those with a significant impact on the success of your personal and professional growth. In doing so, you demonstrate that you are worthy of the same, so both parties can cooperatively mobilize that confidence to progress. It is a comprehensive, all-encompassing, and motivational guide that harnesses some of the greatest minds in business, psychology, neuroscience, and behavioral therapy. The book's mission is to illuminate the path to forging bonds with those that will propel you towards achievement, self-fulfillment and happiness.

Aimee Tariq is a Wall Street Journal Bestselling Author and USA Today Bestselling Author of *Panic! Germs and the Truth Inside American Mouths*. As a pioneer in the health and coaching space, Aimee has helped thousands to harmonize health and wealth. She is a contributor to many large publications such as Entrepreneur Magazine and was quoted by Forbes as a Top 20 Entrepreneur. Aimee is trusted by the leading physicians in the field such as the founder of Holistic Medicine and the president of biological dentistry.

Lisa Fei is the founder and CEO of Clarity, a relationship wellness app designed to build happier and more fulfilling relationships grounded in trust. She is a frequent contributor to major publications such as Entrepreneur Magazine and has been featured in Forbes, USA Today, Business Insider, and many others. Lisa has made it her life's mission to empower others to improve the quality of their personal lives and mental health through healthy, meaningful, and lasting relationships.

Imran Tariq is CEO of Webmetrix Group, a leading public relations and reputation management firm, and quoted in Forbes as a Top 20 Entrepreneur. He has been interviewed on CNN and CNBC and is a frequent guest on TV for his expertise in Google My Business Optimization. He is a contributor to Entrepreneur Magazine, Business Insider, Techcrunch, and many other large publications. Imran has raised hundreds of millions of dollars for businesses all using the power of trust. Thanks to the support of his wife Aimee, he has overcome insurmountable odds.

Tyler Wagner is founder of Authors Unite, a publishing company that has helped thousands of people become Amazon,

THE PYRAMID OF TRUST

Barnes & Noble, USA Today, Wall Street Journal, and New York Times Best Selling Authors. Tyler's hands-on approach guides writers throughout the process of writing, publishing, and successfully marketing their books. He is also the host of the Authors Unite Show and has interviewed over 1,300 renowned thought leaders and entrepreneurs like Gary Vaynerchuk.

BIBLIOGRAPHY

Lewicki, Roy J, Chad T Brinsfield. "(PDF) Framing Trust: Trust as a Heuristic." ResearchGate. Peter Lang Publishing. January, 2011. https://www.researchgate.net/publication/309107248_Framing_trust_trust_as_a_heuristic.

"10 Ways to Show Compassion: Independence University." Go to Independence University. https://www.independence.edu/blog/ways-of-showing-compassion.

Balsamo, Michael. "Ponzi Schemer Bernie Madoff Dies in Prison at 82." AP NEWS. April 15, 2021. https://apnews.com/article/bernie-madoff-dead-9d9bd8065708384e0bf0c840bd1ae711.

Broster, Alice. "How To Improve Your Relationship Based On Your Love Language." TheList.com. March 11, 2021. https://www.thelist.com/353281/how-to-improve-your-relationship-based-on-your-love-language/.

Carlson, Nicholas. "Marissa Mayer Is Late All The Time." Business Insider. January 23, 2013. https://www.businessinsider.com/marissa-mayer-has-a-bad-habit-of-being-late-all-the-time-2013-1.

Chapman, Gary D., and Amy Summers. *The Five Love Languages: How to Express Heartfelt Commitment to Your Mate.* LifeWay Press, 2016.

"Cheating in a Relationship and What Causes Them." FrackingFreeIreland. November 20, 2019. https://frackingfreeireland.org/cheating.

Duncan, Tracey Anne. "Do Love Languages Actually Matter? Psychologists Weigh in." Mic. November 10, 2020. https://www.mic.com/p/do-love-languages-actually-matter-psychologists-weigh-in-18799908.

Frost, P., J. Dutton, Sally Maitlis, Jacoba M. Lilius, Jason Kanov, and Monica C. Worline. "[PDF] Seeing Organizations Differently: Three Lenses on Compassion: Semantic Scholar." Undefined. January 01, 1970. https://www.semanticscholar.org/paper/Seeing-organizations-differently:-Three-lenses-on-Frost-Dutton/45adac0f9dad41b9ff562b50a30a6f3dfb25cd23?p2df.

Lginzy. "How Mark Cuban Started with Just $60 in His Pocket and Became a Billionaire." CNBC. November 28, 2017. https://www.cnbc.com/2017/07/05/how-mark-cuban-became-a-billionaire.html.

Maltz, Maxwell. *Psycho-cybernetics: A New Technique for Using Your Subconscious Power.* Wilshire Book, 1967.

Mark Manson. "The Cognitive Biases That Make Us All Terrible People." Mark Manson. January 16, 2021. https://markmanson.net/cognitive-biases-that-make-us-terrible#actor-observer-bias.

Maslar, Dawn. *Men Chase, Women Choose: The Neuroscience of Meeting, Dating, Losing Your Mind, and Finding True Love.* Health Communications, 2016.

Mayer, Roger C., James H. Davis, and F. David Schoorman. "An Integrative Model Of Organizational Trust." *Academy of Management Review* 20, no. 3 (1995): 709-34. doi:10.5465/amr.1995.9508080335.

McKay, Sarah. *The Women's Brain Book: The Neuroscience of Health, Hormones and Happiness.* Hachette, 2019.

The Merriam-Webster's Dictionary. Merriam-Webster, 2005.

Peter Shallard. "Why You Do Not Trust Yourself." Peter Shallard. May 21, 2019. https://www.petershallard.com/why-you-dont-trust-yourself/.

Rimm, Hannah. "14 Long-Lasting Celebrity Couples Who Will Restore Your Faith in Love." Allure. October 11, 2018. https://www.allure.com/gallery/best-celebrity-couples-long-lasting.

Rivas, Daniel. "Words of Affirmation: How to Speak Your Client's Love Language." Medium. December 04, 2019. https://digitalmedianinja.medium.com/words-of-affirmation-how-to-speak-your-clients-love-language-5e6cf13db9cf.

Solbrig, Linda, Ben Whalley, David J. Kavanagh, Jon May, Tracey Parkin, Ray Jones, and Jackie Andrade. "Functional Imagery Training versus Motivational Interviewing for Weight Loss: A Randomised Controlled Trial of Brief Individual Interventions for Overweight and Obesity."

International Journal of Obesity 43, no. 4 (2018): 883-94. doi:10.1038/s41366-018-0122-1.

"To Build Trust, Competence Is Key." Harvard Business Review. July 23, 2014. https://hbr.org/2012/03/to-build-trust-competence-is-k.

"Vasopressin." Drugs and Lactation Database (LactMed) [Internet]. December 03, 2018. https://www.ncbi.nlm.nih.gov/books/NBK500651/.

"Why Communication Is So Important for Leaders." CCL. March 12, 2021. https://www.ccl.org/articles/leading-effectively-articles/communication-1-idea-3-facts-5-tips/.